PRAISE FOR *ADDING A LITTLE LEVITY*

"In today's world of uncertainty and weighty decisions, *Adding A Little Levity*, is the perfect bedtime read. A chapter a night will leave you smiling, as you drift off into a peaceful sleep. The problem is—you'll be chuckling in your dreams."
Sally Fernandez, Author of the "Max Ford Thriller" Series.

• • •

"I see a lot of wit bubbling away here and an eye for the farcical nightmare."
Arthur Plotnik, Best Selling Author of "Spunk & Bite"

• • •

"Having a tough day? *Adding a Little Levity* is just what the doctor ordered. Bob's essays showcase his observational humor and dry wit about a kid from Queens and his escapades (and cringeworthy blunders) in corporate America and beyond. Sure to put a smile on your face and a spring in your step."
Erin Moran McCormick, Author, "Year of Action"

BLUE STAR
PRESS

Copyright © 2018 Robert J. Licalzi
Published by Blue Star Press
Bend, OR 97708
contact@bluestarpress.com | www.bluestarpress.com

ISBN 978-1944515553

This book is dedicated to my wife, Diane, and my four children, Roberto, Diana, Daniela, and Carolina, whose laughter at some of the earlier essays spurred me on to compose a few more.

ROBERT J. LICALZI

ADDING A
LITTLE LEVITY

ESSAYS TO LIGHTEN A TOUGH DAY

CONTENTS

SECTION 3

WHEN THE GOING GETS WEIRD, THE WEIRD TURN PRO

PREFACE

Make a person smile and you have done well; but make a person laugh out loud and you have achieved something. This book started as a single, light-hearted essay, *Hotel California,* which extracted a few spontaneous laughs, causing those who read it in public places to appear batty. After hearing that, how does one not continue? I recognized that real-life experiences and observations, leavened with a helping of hyperbole, often produce the most humorous results.

So, I wrote a few more essays. Not everyone thought they were funny, but enough people did, spurring me on to fill up this book. My goal is a modest one: to have every person, patient enough to read the entire book, experience, at least once, the enjoyment of unintentionally and heartily laughing out loud.

At home, my dad would always look for opportunities to keep things light, kidding, but never wounding all those around him. He had a special skill. He would defend his playful actions saying that he was trying to "add a little levity to the situation," and unknowingly provided me with an easy choice for the title to this book. Hopefully, this collection of essays will do what its title promises.

—RJL

SECTION 1

EVERYTHING YOU ALWAYS WANTED TO KNOW ABOUT GROWING UP IN QUEENS VILLAGE, NEW YORK, BUT WERE AFRAID TO ASK.

Some people are born on third base and think they hit a triple. I was born in the bleachers and was thrilled I had snuck into the ballpark.

ADVENTURES
IN DINING

I grew up in a family of modest means; my brother, sister, and I learned that nothing was to be wasted, particularly food. Even the hungriest dog would be disappointed looking for food scraps in our garbage. For us, "leftovers" was the name of a meal, no different from a bologna sandwich or a meatloaf (and we all fervently hoped the "meat" in the loaf was beef). We accepted that our low-priced chopped meat contained 35 percent filler—ground bones, cartilage, knuckles generously seasoned with aged offal. It was the 65 percent labeled "meat" we feared.

I remember that by my early teenage years, the quality of our chopped meat improved, perhaps because my father received a salary increase. Although the "meat" portion was as mysterious as ever, and the percentage of filler was the same, it was now ground up more finely. After that, we chewed our meat with greater confidence, knowing that those more-than-occasional, pebble-sized, tooth-chipping, bone fragments were no longer lurking.

We had difficulty containing our excitement surrounding the semi-annual trip to a restaurant. We never knew precisely when this momentous occasion would occur, but my brother and I could deduce that it was a couple of weeks away when our meal portions at home were reduced by half. And when the half-portions were replaced by gruel, we knew it was just a matter of days.

Not wishing to waste his hard-earned money, my dad made sure we were sufficiently hungry so as to fully appreciate our dining-out experience. Because my mom and sister never finished their restaurant meals, and my father had a no-leftovers policy, my dad, brother, and I knew we would have to clean their plates as well. For my father, a doggy bag was not an option. As a matter of honor, we had to eat everything we ordered. He would no sooner skip out of the restaurant in a tutu with a tulip in his ear than he would walk out of there with a doggy bag. "And besides," my dad would say, putting a finer point on it, "We don't own a dog."

Finally, the day arrived. My brother and I were assisted by my mom and younger sister, weakened as we were by the previous period of undernourishment and unable to walk unaided. As we arrived at the restaurant, they helped us to the table, propping us up in our chairs, hoping we wouldn't embarrass them by tipping over. At this point, we followed to the letter, the restaurant routine set by our dad years before. Before any conversation commenced, the first order of business was to consume the entire bread basket. This was perfectly okay for my brother and me, given that we lacked a sufficient amount of stored glycogen to power the mouth and throat muscles required for speech.

Partway through appetizers, though, our ravenous appetites were unleashed. Our pallor was erased, and we gazed covetously at the plates of my mom and sister. Dad ordered a third basket of bread and another family-sized dish of vegetables. Appetizers finished, we were giddy with anticipation as we watched the generous main courses being served to tables around ours. At last, our meals arrived, and we were not disappointed. Huge chunks of fish or meat were accompanied by GMO-sized baked potatoes hidden beneath an improbable amount of butter and sour cream. With a predatory eye on my sister's plate, I told her that she couldn't finish her meal in ten sittings much less one. Dad ordered a fourth basket of bread. We dug in.

About three-quarters through my meal, common sense and a pronounced ache in my stomach told me I'd had enough, but not willing to disappoint my dad, I dared not slow down. With the knowledge that I would also have to eat whatever my sister left, I stopped taunting her and instead began to encourage her to eat more. After a few more agonizing bites of my own, I resorted to begging. I offered to carry her book bag to school every day for two weeks.

Feeling like Joey Chestnut at hotdog number sixty, I finished what was left on my plate, my sister's plate, and the remaining rolls in the fourth bread basket. The ensuing state of gluttonous lassitude was not going to be eased by loosening a belt or unbuttoning a button or two. Involuntarily, conversation stopped, movement ceased, and even breathing abated as our brains shut down all bodily functions not directly related to the digestive challenge at hand. When my sister expressed a possible interest in ordering dessert, which she was unlikely to finish, I had just enough energy to whisper to her that such a decision would put her collection of stuffed animals in grave danger. She passed on dessert.

As we struggled to lift our distended bodies from the table, rising unsteadily, toppling our chairs as we stood, my brother and I once again leaned on my mother and sister for help getting to the car, which now seemed much farther away than I had remembered.

• • •

THE
INTERVIEW

At last, I secured my first interview with a Wall Street bank, Irving Trust, a renowned presence in finance at the time. Never mind the long odds of a red-blooded Italian American gaining entry into a blue-blooded WASPy company. I wasn't even sure how I got the interview. Something on my résumé must have caught their eyes, so it appeared that the extra time I spent preparing it had paid off. I had a hard time deciding whether to feature my education (an economics degree from Queens College, which would appear at the top of the *Princeton Review of College Rankings* if the list started from the bottom), or my primary work experience (a summer newspaper-delivery route).

I figured the Ivy League human resources director sifting through the résumés did not know anything about either one and would be intrigued enough to grant an interview to find out. I also had been careful to beef up my activity list to highlight a second-place finish in softball intramurals during my sophomore year of high school and the trophy I won for bowling a 150 in sixth grade. In the skills section, in an attempt to convey my competence with electronics, I mentioned that I was pretty good at jiggling the vacuum tubes in the back of the family black-and-white TV set in order to steady the picture. I ended the résumé with a list of my interests, including shuffleboard and Bingo.

My first order of business for the interview was to select one of the two suits I owned: the blinding, lime-green, flared-bottom stunner or the light-brown, large-glen-plaid, executive look with the more modestly flared bottoms. I chose the brown plaid for two reasons: I thought the conservative bell-bottom would be a more appropriate match with Wall Street's orthodoxy, and the suit better complemented my clay-brown shoes with the reserved but unmistakable platform heels.

The John Travolta, *Saturday Night Fever* culture had long since petered out throughout the country, but it lingered in the remote corner of Queens, where I lived, which was always a disco twirl or two behind the mainstream in nearly everything.

A couple of days before the interview, I was advised that it would be conducted over lunch at the bank's officers' dining room. Now, I was convinced that the brown plaid suit was the right choice for this setting. I couldn't figure out what warranted such VIP treatment, though. Could it be that the human resources director liked Bingo, too?

Soon the day arrived, and I met the two gentlemen from Irving Trust who would lunch with me and conduct the interview: Thaddeus Lodge III and Nathaniel Poindexter IV. Or was it Lodge IV and Poindexter III? What's with these numbers, anyway? I thought names only contained letters; nobody I knew in Queens had any numbers in their names. The dining room was an elevator ride and a walk down a long corridor from where we met.

The three of us struggled to make small talk, quickly realizing the impossibility of finding anything in common. What I most remember is that the corridor wasn't carpeted, so my wooden-heeled platforms, chirping like crickets, announced my arrival to all the bankers nearby. Thad and Nate's Gucci loafers, on the other hand, glided noiselessly down the hall. I arrived at the dining room with a stiff neck. Lodge III was six foot two, while Poindexter IV was six foot four (or was it Lodge who was six foot four and Poindexter six foot two?).

I had been looking up the entire time since I met them. As if I weren't making enough noise, walking while craning my neck added a decibel or two to my platforms' recital.

We arrived at the dining room, hushed-toned and funereal. Everyone was dressed in dark gray or black pinstripes with odd folds (which I would learn later were called cuffs) at the bottom of their pants. I strained mightily to spot some plaid, but to no avail. I also noticed quite a few bankers straining to see me. *Yup*, I thought as I sauntered in, *you guys might be seeing a lot of me around here after I nail this interview.* But now, it was time to enjoy a free gourmet meal in an upscale dining room.

To show my interviewers that I was health-conscious, I ordered fish, and because I was hungry, I ordered a whole flounder—I didn't want just part of one. I only learned several years later what the word "filet" meant. As it turned out, the meal was the most challenging part of the interview. No matter how carefully I removed the spine from the fish on my plate, each mouthful of flounder was riddled with bones.

I faced a Hobson's choice. Should I pick the bones out of each bite, piling up several fine linen napkins next to my plate, or should I simply chew and swallow the bones, hoping that the two self-absorbed nabobs at my table would not notice? I chose the latter. Despite my masticating with abandon, the bony detritus in each gulp scratched their way down my throat and esophagus, setting both on fire.

Desperate for relief, I downed glass after glass of water. The waiter grew so tired of refilling my glass that he finally brought two pitchers and simply sat down and joined us. I sensed that the banker with the aquiline nose (who had been looking down it at me since we met) was beginning to suspect my attempt at deception. With my discomfort increasing with each bite, I found that I could not remember the interviewers' names; I began calling them Nathaddeus and Thaniel. (Who has names like those anyway? The kids I grew up with were named Stewie, Mikey, and Gino.)

By this time, though, my bladder, overwhelmed by the onrush of water, was giving me a clear signal of distress. I tried to act nonchalant, but concentrating on the questions of Hideous and Neanderthal (I no longer had any idea what their names were) was a challenge. I would have excused myself to go to the men's room, but that required a perp-type walk across the entire carpet-less dining room. By now, even I had figured out that my unique attire was of great interest to the homogeneous collection of Irving Trust funeral directors dining around us. I wouldn't exactly be presenting them with a "Where's Waldo" challenge. So, I remained at the table, where the more I tried to ignore my distended bladder, the more everything around me resembled a urinal. The Righteous Brothers ran out of questions and began to converse with each other about their favorite sport: polo. I was thinking about joining their conversation to talk about mine— stickball—but sensed that it might be too difficult to explain.

Mercifully, lunch ended quickly. I said goodbye to my hosts and disappeared into the nearest elevator. Fortunately, it was empty, so I was able to begin extracting the remaining bones still lodged in my throat. Now, all I needed was a bathroom.

• • •

ANCHORS
AWEIGH

I was born and raised in Queens Village, New York, a long way from the ocean's edge. Maybe once a summer, my father would stuff our family of five into his compact car and drive the twenty miles for a day at the beach. You could say that we were not "water people."

Fast forward years later. At age twenty-nine, having never been on a boat and having barely mastered the dog paddle, I moved to Puerto Rico. A couple of years after that, while I was courting my future wife, Diane, her father, Vic, invited me on board his fifty-foot sailboat along with ten other family members for a weeklong trip around the Caribbean islands.

If there was one person to be marooned with on a deserted island, Diane's father would be a hands-down choice. Tough and with boundless energy, he knew how to fish, farm, sail, and he could fix or build almost anything—he was modern-day Tarzan at home in any of nature's settings or circumstances.

Vic spent his youth collecting outdoor experiences and wrestling with Mother Nature. I spent mine collecting postage stamps. I hoped opposites would attract.

We all met at the marina, unpacked our cars, and walked to the docked sailboat. Everyone carried their belongings in soft, stowable backpacks and duffle bags. I wheeled my gear in a hard, Samsonite suitcase. With many people to impress, I boarded the sailboat with my mouth exceptionally dry and my forehead and underarms sweating more than was warranted by the outside temperature. Because there was little in my stamp-collecting experience that prepared me for the operation of a sailboat, I met Vic on deck for a briefing.

First, I learned that nearly everything on a sailboat has a special name. Concepts like right and left, front and back—universally understood by man since he emerged from a cave, needing to be able to communicate location to his fellow caveman as they stalked the main course for their Paleo diet—are not good enough for a sailboat. Instead, right and left are starboard and port (or is it port and starboard?) and front and back are bow and stern. I looked up stern in the dictionary; the aftermost part of the vessel. I thought dictionaries were supposed to help. Aftermost? Nobody I know on land has ever used that word. Getting on a crowded bus, does the driver tell you, "I think there are some empty seats in the aftermost?" When describing a car accident, does anyone ever say, "I was stopping for a red light when the car behind me smashed into the aftermost part of my car?"

Before I had fully memorized the parts of the boat, Vic began explaining the use of the thousand or so ropes on board, at least half of them requiring a unique knot. He patiently showed me how to tie each knot and then tested me, but other than the one I use for my shoelaces, I wasn't able to tie any of the knots twice in a row. I needed to find some other way to impress him.

Overloaded with instructions on sails, ropes, and knots—few of which I retained—I was next led below deck to learn the operation of the toilet. Located in a room I would have called a broom closet rather than a bathroom, the toilet stared at me imperiously, with an array of buttons and pumps, taunting me to master its use. One button—to be pressed three times—injected a fluid that treated the waste left in the toilet. A second button released water and was not to be pressed more than four times, because we had a limited supply of water on board; a third button flushed the waste away. Oh, and don't flush used toilet paper (Odd. I thought toilet paper was named that for a reason). Instead, toss it into the small plastic container on the floor next to the toilet. Now, between the toilet and this container, there was just enough floor space left for one's feet. Maneuvering inside this room was a challenge. One errant move and you might find your foot inside the plastic bin, something I successfully avoided on most of my visits.

The bathroom was adjacent to the dining table, separated from the last seat at that table by a wooden wall thin enough to ensure that anyone sitting on the toilet wouldn't miss a word of the dinner conversation taking place. At one point, I believe the toilet was part of the dining table seating, the wall having been added later on. This "familiarity," along with my waning confidence that I would have any chance of remembering the bathroom rules, made me resolve to time my bathroom use when everyone was on deck.

Gear stowed, instructions given, Vic navigated the sailboat out of the marina and into the open water using the boat's motor until he detected sufficient wind. The skies were blue, the sun shone, the sea was calm, with gently rolling waves rocking the boat up and down and side to side. After several minutes, Vic announced that we were setting sail, reminding all of us of our tasks.

With speed, energy, and coordination, each family

member scurried about, tying and untying ropes, avoiding moving beams, winching, and grabbing the helm. I had intended to do my part but remained inert. My breakfast reminded me that it hadn't been properly digested. Not at all happy with the undulations since departure, it threatened to reappear. Hopefully, everyone was too busy to notice.

After about an hour of sailing and straining to be part of the group, I sat up for the first time and uttered a full sentence— either not loud enough for anyone to hear, or of little interest. I must have sat up too abruptly. My dizziness reasserted itself, and I returned to the supine position on a bench at the back, (ahem, stern) of the boat.

At last, the waves subsided, a signal that we were nearing land and the cove where we would anchor for the rest of the day and night. The moment the boat was secure, I saw the family hurtling through the air from all directions, diving from elevated parts of the boat, the names of which I had long since forgotten. Never having entered water by any means other than wading, I found the boat's ladder and descended quietly.

Once I was in, Diane invited me to join the group free-diving for conch. This activity seemed to be as much about collecting conch for lunch as it was a competition to see who could dive the deepest on a single breath. I was eager to participate, but after a mild sinus irritation two months before, I was under doctor's orders not to get my hair wet.

When we had our fill of swimming and diving (or ladder-climbing, in my case), Vic suggested that we go to shore to hunt land crabs. I wished aloud that I had packed my butterfly net, but

Vic told me he didn't use any equipment. Not having ever seen one of these crustaceans, I was struck both by their swiftness and the size of their castration-grade claws.

Vic brought us to one of their holes (caves would be a more accurate description of the home of these giants) to demonstrate his technique. He explained that the crab will always sit at the back (aftermost) of the hole facing outward. Knowing this, he reached into the hole, keeping his hand open and flush against the sidewall of the hole. When his hand was behind the sitting crab, he snatched it from behind and brought it out. Crab salad tonight! Coincidentally, just as Vic was about to have me try my luck at the next crab hole, I began to sneeze with uncommon frequency and was forced to return to the sailboat for some Benadryl.

We reassembled on the boat and dug into our first lunch together. Before we finished, I was overcome by an untimely but implacable urge to move my bowels. I excused myself and walked the eighteen inches or so from my seat at the dining table to the toilet. It was a particularly tumultuous and gaseous session. All efforts at noise control on my part were fruitless. I held in a sneeze, only to hear everyone at the table say, "God bless you." Embarrassment turned to panic when, confronting the confusing array of pumps and buttons, I noticed the abnormally large contents I left behind in this undersized toilet bowl. After filling the plastic container to the brim with used toilet paper, I planned my assault on the toilet.

Did I treat first and then pump water, or pump water then treat? How many pumps of each? I couldn't remember what to do but knew that if I weren't successful soon, then the odor, like the noise, would depart from the bathroom and descend like a miasma on the dining table. I pumped, treated, and flushed furiously. I knocked over the plastic container in the process, only to see the toilet contents unmoved.

With whatever dignity I could muster, I asked for help. Vic came in, scooped out the contents from the toilet bowl, and threw it overboard, with me, I was quite certain, soon to follow.

• • •

DRILL,
BABY, DRILL

Outside or inside, Milton Figenbaum always wore sunglasses, which would be problematic if he were a surgeon or a dentist. He was a dentist. And he wasn't just any dentist; he was my family's dentist. My dad, attracted by Milton's low prices, first took me, at age six, to see Doctor Figenbaum and insisted that I go every six months thereafter.

Doctor Figenbaum had his office in one of the smaller rooms of his four-and-a-half room apartment. Since this room was small and Dr. Fig was not, a standard-sized dentist chair wouldn't fit. The clever doctor instead found a chair that didn't recline, sized to accommodate a prepubescent child. I remember having difficulty getting out of that chair and office from nine years old on, and I mark that time as the onset of the claustrophobia from which I suffer today.

Every bit of wall space was covered by sagging shelves, overloaded with dental tools, every mold he had ever taken of his patients, and part of the pastrami sandwich he hadn't finished last week. In fact, there were food scraps everywhere, causing me to wonder whether the Food and Drug Administration had been in there recently to perform an inspection. I was startled when I first saw a rat traversing the shelves, helping clear away scattered comestibles. Doctor Figenbaum assured me that Willard was domesticated and harmless. To the left, was a small window, but because the sill was piled high with more molds, only a few rays of natural light ever came through. I strained to find a diploma of some kind, but of course, there was no available wall space to hang one—assuming he had one to hang—only those menacing shelves, threatening to collapse onto anyone unlucky enough to be trapped in the chair at the time.

Milton's genius in underpricing his competition stemmed from keeping costs low. Unlike other dentists, he never used anesthesia; he never needed to. When it came time to drill a cavity, out came the "high speed" drill, which emitted a noxious odor that knocked the patient unconscious. Because the door between the office and the waiting area didn't seal properly—wait a minute; there was no door— everyone in the waiting area lost consciousness as well. When Doctor Figenbaum awoke, it was usually time for everyone to go home.

I had thought that somewhere on one of those shelves there might be equipment to clean teeth. But no, Milton's approach to dental hygiene was to hand out toothpaste and toothbrushes, many of them in their original packaging. Also notable by its absence was an X-ray machine; there was no room for it anyway. Doctor Figenbaum searched for cavities by turning out the lights, grabbing a flashlight, and asking the patient to open wide. Over his sunglasses, he put the 3D glasses he received at the movie theater showing of *Creature from the Black Lagoon*. He was very good at keeping his balance, stumbling only a few times against the base of the chair before finding my mouth.

In a few short minutes, he located my teeth, and his search for cavities began. I was too young to know where silver for fillings came from, but on one of the back shelves, I did notice some empty gefilte fish cans with tiny holes in them, remarkably similar in size to fillings. One day when I had three teeth filled, I spotted three new holes in one of the cans.

Milton's wife, Hilda, would come into his office every ten minutes or so, usually to bring him lunch and snacks, but mostly to verbally lacerate him, reminding him of how little he earned. Milton's drill hand was noticeably less steady and his drilling more erratic after each of Hilda's visits. One time, I was the last patient of the day. As I left the office to walk home, I could hear, from a distance, Hilda's rantings escalate in both volume and frequency. Then I faintly heard the buzz of the high-speed drill, which puzzled me because all the patients had gone home. I paused for a moment when both the drill and Hilda went quiet. Then, looking back toward the office, I saw Doctor Figenbaum closing the office door behind him with a twinkle in his eye, and a sly, satisfied grin on his face.

Milton loved to talk and insisted on telling me his life story. It was difficult to say I wasn't interested when the good dentist had my mouth jammed open with one of the clamps he retrieved from the shelf with the gefilte fish cans. He was an intimidating figure with his 3D glasses, which he had forgotten to remove after the X-ray session. My intimidation turned into white-knuckle fear when I saw a drill in his hand and the 3D glasses still on his nose. To his credit, he never drilled more than a couple of teeth before finding the correct one.

Perhaps sensing that I was unnerved by the abundance of shelving and absence of diplomas, Doctor Figenbaum recounted his past. A Russian by blood and birth, he graduated from Murmansk Community College, where he had a dual major in dentistry and strip mining. Normally a six-year program of study—the first two years devoted to strip mining and the last four years to dentistry—it was reduced to two years because, as it was a time of war, there was a shortage of dentists, most of them having been sent to fight at the Russian front. Luckily for Milton, he was granted a military deferment for flat feet, allowing him to start his dentistry practice after two years.

Milton's father, well-connected in the Communist Party, had been a cook for the Bolsheviks during the Revolution. His culinary specialty, which he named Beef Stroganoff, almost got him executed when Lenin complained of an upset stomach. Milton ran into problems of his own when his father recommended him to fill an aching cavity for Sergei Alexandrovich. Milton's father knew Alexandrovich from the days of the Revolution when Sergei had been Lenin's barber. Sergei lived in constant fear that he had taken too much off the top. But his meticulous trimming enabled him to rise through the ranks, eventually becoming a member of the Politburo, as well as its barber. Milton examined Sergei, and, as would plague Milton throughout his professional career, he mistakenly drilled the wrong tooth, leaving Sergei with two toothaches instead of one. Milton was dispatched to a Siberian gulag and sentenced to five years of hard labor.

Ever resourceful, Milton avoided being assigned strenuous tasks by giving clinics to the guards on the importance of daily flossing. He further improved the quality of his life and secured extra food rations in return for demonstrating to the guards methods of flattening their feet to avoid military service. Most of Milton's work was outdoors in the Siberian snow, where the glare of the sun weakened his eyes. This explained the sunglasses he had to wear indoors and out later in life, but not necessarily his habitual inability to find the correct tooth to drill. Milton's foot-flattening lessons weren't working; every week, a few more guards were dragged off to the front. After nine months, there were no more guards left, so Milton packed his belongings and simply walked out of the gulag. He caught a train to Murmansk, hoping to complete his dentistry degree. He found, though, that his college had been converted, out of wartime necessity, to a delicatessen dedicated to providing take-out orders for the troops at the front. He joined the deli, and thanks to Milton, it became famous for its borscht.

When war ended, Milton married Hilda (who had been in charge of pickles at the deli), and they moved to the United States, where they opened a deli specializing in pickled borscht. When that enterprise failed, Milton had no option but to open a dentistry practice and begin the on-the-job training he had never received.

By the time Doctor Figenbaum finished his story, nightfall had arrived, I had fallen asleep, all of the waiting patients had gone home, no money had been made, and Hilda was furious. Because no work had actually been done on my teeth, I made another appointment for the following week.

Once I arrived at the appointed time and squeezed into the dentist chair, the forgetful Doctor Figenbaum asked me if I had heard his life story.

• • •

LATE TO
THE ALTAR

No, I wasn't late to the altar on the day of my wedding.
I just took a great deal of time finding someone to marry. I
celebrated my thirty-ninth birthday having—to the chagrin of my
long-suffering mother, desperate for grandchildren—no prospects
in sight. I learned from a neighbor that my mom had been
visiting a fertility clinic, figuring that her chances of becoming a
grandmother were better if she started over with a new child of
her own.

I dated regularly throughout my adult life, but as the cliché
goes, the right girl just wasn't coming along. It didn't help that
I had become more exacting as is natural with advancing age.
To this, I had the added concern about potential gold diggers,
particularly after my recent promotion to co-assistant manager at
the local Dairy Queen.

I had been making a concerted effort to date older,
financially self-sufficient women, who were less likely to have
designs on my nest egg and hopefully more interested in who I
was rather than who I had become. Such a woman would likely
be more sophisticated, someone I could be comfortable taking to
a convention of Dairy Queen assistant managers or a business
dinner at Denny's.

One night, a friend invited me to a professional basketball
game and sent my heart racing after introducing me to a very
attractive and sophisticated woman, named Allison Prescott.
Allison had graduated from Miss Porter's School and Harvard,

and she had the type of job in the finance world that could make me relax about protecting my money.

We had a wonderful conversation that night, although I now recall that I did most—or was it all?—the talking. I had trouble contacting Allison over the next few days, and I asked my friend to find out if she had any interest in me. Allison told him she was allergic to ice cream. Poor girl. A life without ice cream was a burden too painful to imagine.

I never wanted to be a trophy husband, nor was I interested in acquiring a trophy wife, although I was once tempted. At a county fair, I was introduced to, and immediately smitten by, Margaret Elmendorf, partly because she was young and pretty, but mostly because of her position as manager of the local Outback Steakhouse. Being in the food service business myself and knowing how difficult it is to rise through the ranks, I was impressed with the level she had achieved at such a young age.

We chatted a bit, but my nervousness caused my tongue to malfunction and made me sound both unintelligible and unintelligent. I allowed myself to daydream about dining with her at the Outback, at an employee's discount, then proudly moving over to Dairy Queen for dessert, also at an employee's discount. My reverie was interrupted by the arrival of her husband, who was making a triumphant return from the pig races, where his entrant had won.

Not long after, I met Emma Pearson, who had moved to the United States from Great Britain on a job assignment a couple of years earlier. She was good-looking, very reserved, and I loved her accent. After a couple of dates, I brought her to my friend Joe's house for a Sunday barbecue.

Joe was married with two toddlers and at least as many dogs. Emma did her best to hide her revulsion to children and pets, not to mention hamburgers and hot dogs (Oh, because the cuisine in England is good?) We continued to date a few more times, but Emma was Emma, someone who epitomized the typical British caricature, with a stiff upper lip who made rigor mortis sufferers seem ebullient.

Starved of warmth and feeling, I rebounded from Emma with Sunshine Williams. Yes, that was her real name. I met Sunshine at a park, where she was tossing a Frisbee to a dog and playing hide and seek with her sister's young children. She had a pretty face, probably an appealing figure beneath her loose clothing, and most certainly had beautiful hair if it hadn't been affixed in some inscrutable combination of corn rows and dreadlocks. But most of all, she possessed a sensitivity that had been absent in Emma.

We agreed to a date. I thought dinner and a movie would be a promising way to start. I soon found out there wasn't a social itch Sunshine didn't want to scratch: abortion rights, gays in the military, censorship on campuses, people who wear fur coats, climate change, equal rights for men and women. We began seeing each other, but that dinner and movie proved elusive. Our dates— all of which took place at some rally or protest—started with me waving a placard and Sunshine hurling insults, then objects both soft and hard, and ended with us fleeing from horse-mounted police wielding billy clubs.

I endured months of this routine before I realized that Sunshine's sensitivity didn't extend beyond her causes to the men she was dating. I broke up with her and wanted to immediately put that whole experience out of my mind, but couldn't because it took several months to rinse the last bits of pepper spray from my eyes.

I went through a long dry spell before I met Crystal at a bar one night. Having had far too much to drink, I couldn't recall all parts of the evening with equal clarity. I knew I wanted to see Crystal again and vaguely remembered her saying something about tricks, so I concluded that she must be a magician. Excited, I told everyone I knew.

I invited Crystal to dinner at an upscale restaurant to join a friend of mine and his wife. Crystal seemed bewildered by the forks, spoons, and knives in front of her, but I thought nothing of it. After dinner, she lit up a cigarette, prompting the maître d' to quickly appear at our table to discreetly remind her there was no smoking in the restaurant. Just as quickly as he arrived at our table did he depart, scampering away from the verbal abuse directed his way by dear Crystal.

My friend and his wife thought it was a good time to leave the restaurant, excused themselves, and left with exceptional haste. Alone now, Crystal and I walked for a while, and then she asked me what my preferences were. I told her that I preferred the Yankees over the Mets. She kissed me on the forehead, and I never saw her again.

I can't forget my only date with Blake Gordon. Now Blake can be both a girl's name and a boy's name, but it wasn't only her name that I found confusing. She was a likable young lady. We teased each other quite a bit, and the few times we playfully jostled each other, I noted an uncommon degree of strength. We had a pleasant evening, which culminated with a long, sultry kiss goodnight.

I never saw her again after that, although a couple of weeks later, I saw a well-built man with his shirt off operating a jackhammer at a construction site. He had an uncanny resemblance to Blake, and I hoped to God she had a twin brother.

Not often do beauty and brains reside in a single person, but they did in Mackenzie Parker. Her figure and fine features were unquestionably alluring, and she was so smart that I rarely understood what she was talking about. She was preparing several scholarly articles for publication. The two we discussed in detail were: "The Interpretation of the Dreams of Emasculated Men in a Post-Feminist World" and "The Destructive Forces of Chivalry in a Post Post-Feminist World." Mackenzie was a very well-educated young woman, an intellectual who had spent seven years at Smith College to earn her bachelor's degree in militant women's studies. I was willing to discuss any topic that helped me get closer to her.

If it wasn't one of her articles we were discussing, then it was the shortcomings of her psychiatrist, Lazslo, with whom she had a love-hate relationship. As critical as she was about Lazslo, she never made a major (or minor, for that matter) decision without consulting him. Mackenzie was high-strung and disoriented when she faced a decision and he was unavailable. Now that I think about it, she was high- strung and disoriented even when not facing a decision. But her figure explained my persistence. One day, she lambasted me, saying with equal amounts of fury, impatience, and condescension, "Haven't you read Kierkegaard?" And all I had asked her was whether she wanted Italian or Chinese. Anyway, I wasn't sure whether Kierkegaard was the rookie shortstop for the Minnesota Twins or the fellow who piloted the Kon-Tiki, so I simply smiled weakly and didn't respond.

After a couple of tense weeks, Mackenzie began to relax. Our courtship ended after an evening of dinner and a movie with easy conversation and lots of laughs. We walked to her apartment holding hands. I said goodnight and attempted to kiss her, but she recoiled at the strategic moment, saying she would have to ask Laszlo for permission.

Smarting from this rejection and increasingly desperate, I bumped—both figuratively and literally—into Nicolette Wilder. Nicolette was a voluptuous young woman with a chest that demanded attention. I believe that her creator was so focused on crafting a perfect body that he may have overlooked even some basic work on the cranial side of things.

Nicolette wasn't sure which oceans bordered the east and west coasts of the United States. She refused to believe that the Earth was spinning, and while using a compass, thought that north was always the direction in which you were walking. I dated her for a few weeks but never really got a good look at her face. I fantasized about marrying her but concluded I would be forever spilling hot soup on my shirt and tie (assuming she could learn how to prepare soup).

At this point, I clearly needed a change of course. Why not try a dating website? I tried looking at some of the more exotic ones: the Moldavian, Lithuanian, and Mongolian ones, to name a few. But it was through a Latina dating site that I met Beatriz, a Cuban émigré who, I would soon find out, had way more energy than I did. Beatriz—who spent most of her waking hours dancing merengue and salsa—would drag me to obscure clubs in bad neighborhoods where she seemed to know everyone, including the menacing-looking ones.

Being an old-fashioned guy, I am accustomed to the male protecting the female, but I am quite certain that if Beatriz weren't with me, I would have been relieved of both my wallet and my consciousness in a back alley. I wasn't a very good dancer, and my only exposure to merengue and salsa was in a restaurant a few months before. Beatriz, on the other hand, moved with energy, style, and Emilio, her strapping six-foot-three dancing partner, whom she assured me was gay.

She tried showing me the dance steps, without much success, and then pleaded, "Allow Emilo to teach you." Exhausted, I reluctantly agreed. Cheek to cheek and holding hands, Emilio led me through the salsa and merengue steps. I didn't get any better, and he started to enjoy it too much. Beatriz started to lose her patience, which is something I could ill afford in that neighborhood. I pretended I was feeling queasy, politely excused myself, and left while I still could.

Beatriz made me realize I wasn't in very good shape, so I joined a local gym, where I met Nikki. I don't know what attracts me to fanatical women, but Nikki's gym was Beatriz's dance floor. Nikki was a workout warrior who also professed to be an expert in nutrition. Before long, she was prescribing exercises, foods to eat, foods to avoid, herbs, vitamins, mineral supplements.

Being an assertive (and strong) young woman, she ignored my protests. Weekend nights, when most normal people would be taking in dinner and a movie, found us grunting amorously to each other during bench-press reps. During these torture sessions, I thought of nothing other than the shower that followed and a good meal at a nice restaurant. But Nikki, who didn't trust restaurant food, insisted on cooking for me whenever we were together. Every meal seemed to be the same—suma root, sprouted mung beans, wheatgrass, chia seeds, and something that looked like insect larvae. Only the relative portions of each changed.

When I complained of early onset dyspepsia, Nikki knew exactly what I needed and prepared several Kohlrabi–Tiger Nut–Cucamelon smoothies, with chia seeds, of course, sprinkled on top. I ignored the occasional feeling of stomach bloat, which coincidentally began on the day I met Nikki, and achieved relief through controlled flatulence. I broke out in hives, especially in the facial area, and no amount of breath mints could protect the people around me from the odor that accompanied my speech. The bloat and flatulence persisted, but my control was unable to keep up. My coworkers at Dairy Queen gently advised that it would be best for me to remain in back and not serve customers at the counter. A couple of days later, they urged me to simply stay home. Nikki redoubled her efforts in the kitchen to devise more poison potions to help me get better. Out of desperation, I declared I was going on a hunger strike to protest the use of genetically modified seeds in our food supply, and after three short months, she lost interest and left me.

At last I found someone who had an interest in restaurants, probably because she was so young that she hadn't been to many. Based on her behaviors and speaking patterns, Sarah must have been a post-post Millennial. She had a vocabulary all her own and was able to chew gum, without removing it, straight through a three-course meal.

One evening, when we were deciding on a restaurant for dinner, she mentioned Luigi's. She said the food was sick, the chef was insane, the decor was filthy, and the specials were random. I told her I didn't want to spend good money on food that might make us ill, made more likely if the chef was mentally unbalanced and the decor was in need of cleaning. I also preferred that the chef prepare specials according to a recipe rather than randomly. We did go to a restaurant that evening, but Sarah never returned my phone calls after that.

I was fast approaching age forty, had failed to sustain any meaningful relationships, didn't see anyone promising on the horizon, but still hadn't reached rock bottom. That happened after I applied for a spot on The Bachelor TV show. I never received a response, so I waited outside the studio eight hours a day hoping to discuss that oversight directly with the producer. Every day for three weeks, I pestered everyone who went into and came out of the building, inquiring about the producer, until I was arrested for harassment and thrown in jail for a week.

But miracles do happen, and soon after my incarceration ended, I finally met the woman I wanted to marry: Diane. My beleaguered mother was overjoyed and wasted no time checking out of the fertility clinic. Diane and I were married one year later, a full three months after her last homework assignment was due.

• • •

MARATHON
MAN

I was twenty-five years old when running a marathon became my goal. I began training at age forty-five. Some might perceive that as an absence of seriousness, but I had to leave myself sufficient time to learn about marathon training because I knew nothing about it. When I first heard the term carbo-loading, I thought it was a unique method of reloading rifles that helped the Continental Army win the Revolutionary War.

I read extensively during those two decades, learning the importance of nutrition and hydration during exercise of long duration such as a marathon. The normal human body can store enough energy for approximately sixteen to eighteen miles of running and will often shut down or "hit the wall" at that point; hence, the importance of ingesting carbohydrates both before and during the race.

I was determined to avoid ever hitting that wall, so immediately before my first training run, I ate a stack of pancakes smothered in maple syrup. I threw up after the first half-mile. Upon rereading that section more carefully, I noted that the pre-training or pre-race meal should be taken a *few hours* before starting.

Undeterred by this minor setback, I bounded out of the house for my second training run. About three-quarters of a mile away, slightly farther than I had reached the day before, an ornery, snarling dog confronted me. How to deal with ornery, snarling dogs was Chapter Twelve of *How to Train for a Marathon*. I was on Chapter Eleven. Part of the dog's irritability may have stemmed from not having eaten in a while, a hypothesis I was reluctant to test.

I figured I could disarm him by smiling and making some cooing noises, but that only increased his surliness. This canine had mauling on his mind. Walking backward as quickly as I could without being too obvious only insulted his intelligence; he indicated such by revealing even more of his large, shapely, white fangs. I tiptoed to the street corner behind me, and once out of his sight, I sprinted home to safety. I hadn't run that fast since my early teenage years when my Uncle Vito took me along with him to steal hubcaps from police cars.

After concluding that dogs aren't always man's best friend, I suspended my training regimen for several weeks to regain my composure. When I restarted, I moved my training indoors, running several laps around my living room without missing a day. Several months later, I heard that the friendly dog had moved, so I resumed running outside, and within a year I had my mileage up to five plus miles per week. The *How to Train* book said I was a bit behind schedule, but I figured that in just a couple more years, I would be ready to race.

The book also suggested that speed work (i.e., sprints) be included in one's training regimen. The road in front of my house—flat, quiet, and about 150-yards long—was well suited for sprints, and I was eager to begin. I changed into my running gear and walked to the street where, by chance, I met my neighbor. She was a young mother, walking her infant son in a stroller, headed in the same direction as I was. We exchanged pleasantries, I took off, and nearly beat her to the end of the street. Not wishing other people to see my tortoise-like skills, I retreated to my living room to train, doing wind sprints across the entire length of the room, again without missing a day.

At long last, race day was fewer than twenty-four hours away. I reviewed the pre-race checklist, which was burned into my memory: (1) get a good night's sleep, (2) eat a carbohydrate-rich meal a couple of hours prior to the race, (3) have a thorough bowel movement before the race, (4) dress properly for the expected weather conditions.

I climbed into bed early, at 9:30 p.m., and set the alarm for 5:00 a.m., three hours before race time, early enough to eat and digest a substantial pre-race meal. Two hours and 10,000 counted sheep later, I lay staring at several cracks in the ceiling. I got out of bed, ate a snack, read, and watched TV—and remained wide awake. It was well past 2:00 a.m. before the Sandman finally struck, and only two hours later, the alarm reminded me how little I had slept. I felt more like I had just run a marathon than having one to run.

I ate my pre-race meal, headed to the bathroom for the crucial purge of the bowels, and had as much success on the toilet as I had in bed. I pushed so hard that I had to place a couple of fingers on each eyeball to prevent them from popping to the floor on the day of such an important race. So determined was I to continue trying and so intractable was my constipation that I lost track of time. Only twenty-five minutes to race time! With distended bowels, I put on my t-shirt, shorts, socks, and sneakers, dashed into my car, and drove speedily to the race site. The temperature this morning was thirty-five degrees, wind chill around twenty degrees, both of which I had failed to check because of other preoccupations.

As we stood around the starting line waiting for the race to start, I was trying not to attract any attention, hoping no one would notice that I was the only one without sweatpants and a wool cap on this frigid morning. The noise from my chattering teeth—audible to anyone within a hundred yards—betrayed me. My cold-induced stutter made it impossible to have a lucid conversation with anyone around me. I fought to resist the onset of hypothermia, which had already begun to deaden my senses. Fortunately, my hearing was the last to go, so I was able to hear, faintly, the sound of the starting gun. Running helped me beat back the hypothermia. My fingers and toes once again became useful body parts. Nearing the two-mile marker, somewhat earlier than most people, I "hit the wall." Compounding my loss of energy was a warning from my bowels of unfinished business. There were no portable toilets along the way, only at the starting line, so I had to either return to the start or hold it for another twenty-four miles, the latter being about as likely as Uncle Vito getting out of jail early for good behavior.

Back to the start I went, rarely having been so glad to see a Port-o-San. The relief was palpable but short-lived as I realized I still had twenty-six miles to go. Nevertheless, I was again headed in the right direction, running well. To my surprise and smug satisfaction, I began passing several people, even if they were octogenarians and nonagenarians. Midway through the race, I spotted a fleet eighty-eight-year-old grandfather and an opportunity for me to conserve energy by running closely behind him, employing the technique of drafting.

That worked for a while, but I suspect the benefits were minimal after I fell more than a mile behind him. Luck was on my side, though, as a second opportunity to draft—behind Myrtle, a ninety-two-year-old great-grandmother with a walker— appeared with just three miles to go, which eventually brought me to the finish line. As I crossed it, eager to know my race time, I looked for the race clock, but in vain. The race organizers had long ago packed up and gone home.

Myrtle and I will be lodging a formal complaint.

• • •

C U L T U R E
S H O C K

I grew up in a lower-middle class, provincial neighborhood in Queens, New York, where acceptance of diversity eluded some of the residents, particularly those of my parents' generation. Nevertheless, partly because of my awareness of prejudices against my own ethnic group, Italian-Americans, I was a tolerant fellow, certainly by the standards of the day. Heck, I would later make my home in Puerto Rico and marry a Puerto Rican woman. At the time, I knew only two things about Puerto Ricans:

(1) More of them could fit into a Ford Pinto than anyone thought possible. Whenever a car of theirs pulled up to discharge its passengers, I wasn't sure whether my mind was playing tricks on me.

Were the same eight people rotating in and out of the car three times, or were there really twenty-four of them in there? And they could have easily squeezed in another one or two if they were willing to remove the foam dice, baby shoes, rosary beads, and Puerto Rican flags hanging from the rearview mirror.

Their cars always shook when driving, which I first thought was because they weren't tuned well, but subsequently realized it was caused by the sound coming from the Carnegie Hall–sized woofers in the trunk.

(2) They wore impossibly pointy shoes, probably so they could conduct their normal business affairs in case they accidentally left their switchblades at home. When one of them asked for your wallet, they didn't seem to respond to the word, no. Some people thought that they had difficulty understanding English, but I thought it was because their hearing was impaired from frequent rides in Pintos with giant woofers.

So, in my late twenties and with some trepidation, I accepted my employer's job assignment to Puerto Rico. My cultural adventure didn't wait for my arrival on the island. It began on the flight. My fellow passengers included an aggressive-looking young man who sat two rows behind me, in handcuffs, and a semi-toothless gentleman sitting next to me who felt compelled to strike up a conversation by asking me, in broken English, how much I paid for my ticket. Finally, there was the "bring-your-pet-along" discount, which the airline must have been offering, judging by the dozens of clucking chickens on the flight.

Landed, with luggage in tow, I hesitatingly began my new life in Puerto Rico with a smiling taxi cab driver who turned a short ride to my hotel into a long one, charging me accordingly.

Determined to fit in with 98 percent of the population, I purchased a Toyota Corolla. I even tried to mimic their driving style but couldn't adjust the seat backward and downward enough, until I realized that most Puerto Rican drivers had ripped the front seat out and simply sat on the floor. I wondered how they could see where they were going, and such things as stop signs, traffic lights,   and signs directing slow-moving traffic into the right lane. The answer was they couldn't, which made me wish I had bought a larger, safer car.

There was another reason why the purchase of a Corolla was not a smart one, made obvious one morning when I found my car, without tires, sitting on four milk crates. The huge fleet of Corollas on the island required servicing, and many young entrepreneurial Puerto Ricans entered the trade, working the night shift. The silver lining in all of this was that my tire replacement took a couple of days, taking me off the road, where anything goes, and usually does.

Puerto Ricans congenitally drive well in excess of the speed limit, turn on (and leave on) their bright lights from dusk onward, and treat the turn signal stick as if it were coated with the Ebola virus. Lack of driving etiquette? Disrespect for the law? Hardly. Slow down too much, and those parts-seeking entrepreneurs will begin dismantling your Corolla while you are en route to your favorite cockfighting arena. So, the astute Puerto Rican driver will keep those predators distracted with the glare of the high beams and will refrain from using the turn signal to keep them guessing which way they are going.

Full cultural immersion didn't occur until my future wife, Diane, brought me to a party at her home, so I could meet her family. Puerto Ricans need to create a word, in English or Spanish, that refers to that period of time when a party is *not* taking place, not only to round out the lexicon, but to function as an all-clear signal for those of us wishing to avoid at least a few of these fiestas.

The party was in full swing when I arrived. The shouting and music were deafening. People were too numerous for the space available—exactly how I had imagined it being inside a Ford Pinto with woofers. I didn't understand a word anyone was saying, which had little to do with my paucity of Spanish language skills.

No one understood what anyone else was saying because everyone was talking at the same time, several decibels higher than a typical fire alarm. After meeting each of the two hundred people at the party, all of whom were related, I was forced to perform my spasmodic version of salsa and merengue—again and again and again—to the utter delight of all two hundred. No one even pretended to be laughing with me, just at me, and they were not satisfied until all remaining strands of my self-esteem were erased.

With all this "dancing," I was getting hungry. The family eagerly offered me some appetizers, a misnomer if there ever was one, of *cuajo* (pig stomach) and *morcilla* (pig intestine filled with pig blood and rice). Why do they even bother with the rice on that last one? I politely declined, but the others around me couldn't eat the sausage fast enough. Most of it found its way inside their mouths, although some squirted onto their cheeks and chins.

At this very moment, a group of men entered the house playing what I learned later was called Batucada, a relentless, frenzied drumbeat, which provoked images of me simmering in a huge black kettle like Bing Crosby and Bob Hope in *Road to Zanzibar*. I nervously wondered whether this bloodthirsty group, where everyone was related, was ritualistically playing with their food (me on the dance floor) before the final feast. I thought about escape.

Dinner was announced, and although I was hugely relieved to find I was not on the menu, for now, I was never quite sure about later as I watched Diane's family continue to gorge themselves. Once seated, I was confronted by Diane's great aunt, Titi Conchi, carrying a huge pot of food and a ladle capable of knocking me unconscious should she use it for that purpose. Conchi, the family's food warden, would somehow assess my value system and worthiness for entry into the family by my performance at the dinner table.

After serving me mounds of whatever was in that pot—goat, rabbit, and other vermin that Diane refused to reveal to me—she watched and waited for any daylight to appear on my plate. Once she spotted it, the ladle came down with a crash, and a new blob of piping hot stew was stacked precariously on the dish in front of me. This was not a battle I was going to win, but I gamely persisted until my inability to breathe had me begging Diane for a respite, even if it meant a return to the dance floor.

Well, Titi Conchi gave her approval. I married into the family, who gracefully accepted my continued refusal to eat blood sausage. Very quickly, I have found the Puerto Rican culture, customs, and tradition both interesting and endearing. It has been a wonderful time for me, marred only by a recurring dream of being trapped in a black kettle of rapidly warming water.

• • •

A FEW
GOOD MEN

The military exploits of George Washington, Ulysses S. Grant, Robert E. Lee, George Patton, and Dwight Eisenhower, to name a few, were the objects of my fascination as a young boy. If a book wasn't a biography about a military hero, then I didn't read it.

At first, I focused only on the celebrated veterans of American wars but soon became interested in other wars and other countries. Before long, I stumbled upon, and became fixated by books recounting the martial prowess of the Israeli military and the ruthless effectiveness of their national intelligence agency, Mossad, their internal security agency, Shin Bet, and their counter-terrorism unit, Kidon. I learned that three years of military training is mandatory for every Israeli, male or female.

These books made clear that one doesn't mess with the Israelis, which to me, meant anyone who is Jewish. Now, I was confused. I was growing up in a Jewish neighborhood in Queens, New York, and my readings forced me to reassess the parents of all my neighborhood friends. I hadn't realized until then what a fearsome group they were. Not only must they have been exceptionally skilled militarily, but they must have also been brilliantly trained to conceal their ferocity as they settled into nondescript towns and villages like Queens.

Irving Sugarman, my best friend Stewie's father, had trouble walking around the block twice without resting. He didn't seem like much of an athlete, based on the effete way in which he threw a baseball. I remember his playing catch with Stewie one day and lasting only a few throws. He complained of tightness and pain in his right arm, probably aggravating an old injury sustained from tossing hand grenades deep into enemy territory. Irving wore a sling for several months after that. He didn't go to work during this period, though come to think of it, he had never gone to work before that either. Nothing will erase the memory, on those special summer weekends, of watching Irving struggle with his barbecue. He never could manage to ignite the coals, but he was masterful at igniting the fury of his wife, Ethel, whose fiery invective, if directed at the charcoal, would have solved Irving's barbecue problem. Clearly, he was experienced at withstanding orders barked at him by a superior officer. I imagined Irving as a tank driver, with Ethel as tank commander, sitting defiantly atop the tank's turret, scouring the landscape for enemies foolish enough to be within firing range.

Izzy Moskowitz, who lived a couple of doors down from us, seemed to sleep a lot, especially on weekends and the five days between. His wife Ruth and two children said he worked as a mechanic at a gas station, but I never saw him leave the house. I would only see him, on occasion, at his door front—yawning, in pajamas or less, with hair disheveled—when I came calling for his kids to come outside and play. I presumed he must have been assigned often to delicate night operations during his military years and was still catching up on lost sleep.

I never saw Morty Goldfarb, who lived next to the Sugarmans, without a yarmulke bobby-pinned to the side of his head. Morty almost always wore a suit and tie and perpetually seemed to be on his way to the synagogue. Whether he ever got there is anybody's guess.

He never liked to do any chores, which must be the reason he always put on a suit and tie and told anyone near him he couldn't lift anything because of a bad back. Although not as vocal about it, Irving had a similar aversion to lifting things. So, when Morty and Irv faced a task that involved lifting, they called Ethel, who after doing what was asked, unfurled a withering verbal lashing at the two of them. It was painful to watch, but Morty and Irv, whose testicles were largely ornamental, took it in stride. I imagined that Morty was an infantry officer in the Israeli army and may have hurt his back in hand-to-hand combat with some of Israel's most tenacious enemies.

Herbie Silverstein lived in the apartment below us. Unlike Irving and Izzy, Herbie seemed to be working all the time. He left his house before any of us woke and returned home long after we had gone to sleep. His children told me he worked at a factory that made lamps and lighting fixtures, which could have been true because their apartment had five times as many lamps as places to sit.

Herbie was tall but very skinny. His wife, Thelma, was nearly as wide as he was tall. Herbie was a nice enough fellow. He always wore a weak, somewhat goofy smile, and reminded me of a teenager who just completed summer sleep-away camp after winning a half-dozen participation medals. But I had the impression Herbie wasn't very smart. He never spoke very much, while Thelma never stopped.

In fact, I can't recall Herbie ever finishing a sentence. Thelma believed she could better express any thought that may have accidentally entered Herbie's mind. I figured that during his time in the military, Herbie made up for lack of strength with the leverage obtained from his lanky frame. Besides, I guessed that given his expertise with lighting fixtures, he probably headed the interrogation unit in the counter-terrorism agency. I bet more than one terrorist made the mistake of underestimating Herbie before undergoing one of his interrogations.

The last of the fathers living on my block was my friend Jacob's father, Sy Rosenfeld. At first, I mistook Sy for a man of leisure, if for no other reason than I always saw him hanging around dressed in pastel-colored polyester leisure suits. He was no more than five-foot-four-inches tall, and he must have been bald because the hair that sat on the top of his head never looked the same two days in a row. I am not quite sure what happened, but quite suddenly, Sy began working nights and sleeping during the day—or at least trying to since our pickup baseball games were played just outside his apartment window. At first, he would open his window and ask us politely to keep the noise level down, but that proved impossible for us.

Before long, he would appear at his window in an uncontrollable rage, bellowing at us to quiet down, or else. I was young and certainly no doctor, but he seemed to be suffering from distemper, perhaps caused by the bite of an infected dog. Then again, it could have been the flare-up of a condition he had since his military days.

My newfound esteem for my friend's fathers grew with each new book I read about the Israeli military. Knowing they could snap my neck effortlessly, I hesitated to even make eye contact. And I was sure to call all of them sir, especially Ethel.

• • •

PUNITIVE
DAMAGES

Sometimes a guy just can't catch a break.

Murray Lapelowitz and I became good friends growing up in Queens Village, NY. He lived just a few houses away from mine, we attended the same school, and were in some of the same classes. We started to drift apart when I started dating and Murray did not. His name doomed him in two ways.

Murray was always awkward around girls, but I was convinced his name had something to do with it. Murray Lapelowitz was the name of someone forty or more years old. When he was sixteen, eighteen, or twenty years old, Murray had trouble talking to girls his own age, most noticeably after he introduced himself. This continued, well, until Murray was forty years old when he finally grew into his name. Yep, forty years old and never been winked at, much less kissed. That is, until he met Ruthie.

When we were kids, Murray dreamed of being a musician. He didn't play any musical instruments and had no ostensible musical talent, but he certainly did dream a lot. Unfortunately for him, Murray was a Lapelowitz, the scion of a long line of tailors. His great grandfather was a tailor, his grandfather was a tailor, his father was a tailor, two uncles on his father's side were tailors, and two of his cousins were tailors. The Lapelowitz's, perennial fixtures in the community, were known for three generations by everyone who lived along Hillside Avenue between 217th and 221st streets. Murray was whistling Dixie, which he often did, if he thought he would be pursuing music instead of measuring and cutting fabrics for a living.

As expected, Murray entered the family business after graduating from college and began a rigorous fifteen-year apprenticeship program under the tutelage of his Uncle Seymour. The apprenticeship started with measuring cuffs and worked its way up to altering lapels, the Lapelowitz specialty. Uncle Seymour felt Murray needed an additional year of training, but the family convinced him that Murray was now ready to be put in charge of marking garments for alterations.

He and Ruthie met on the eHaberdashers.com dating website, attracted to each other by a mutual interest in Pinpoint Oxford fabric and Mahjong. Murray didn't use these sites very often, but Ruthie did. He could never shake a nagging embarrassment about his name, feeling that it detracted from the image he wished to portray. He still had fleeting hopes of becoming a musician. But whoever heard of a musician named Murray Lapelowitz? He thought seriously about changing his name to Ishmael Lapelowitz but didn't want to risk his family's ire.

After a few days of email, text, and video banter, Ruthie asked Murray to spend a week with her in a cabin in upstate New York. The only time she had available was in three weeks. At last, his luck had turned. The next day at work, Murray exuded a warm glow, was uncharacteristically chatty, and alternatively burst out in throaty laughter, and then in giggles. He had a difficult time concentrating on his work, sticking himself twice with a needle while altering a customer's cuffs, and then piercing the customer's ankle twice during the same fitting. By day's end, Murray would ask Uncle Seymour for vacation for his rendezvous in the woods with Ruthie.

"You can't take that week off," Uncle Seymour said. "It's high hemming season."

Murray pleaded, bribed, and begged his uncle, who eventually relented and gave him the week off. The next day at work, Murray's glow was fiery, he wouldn't shut up, and his immoderate laughing and giggling led to a mild seizure. But Murray was irrepressible. Until he went home that night and found an unusual letter waiting for him.

Murray was being summoned for jury duty by the Federal District Court on the exact day that he was to begin his weeklong getaway with Ruthie. Initially, he brushed it off, confident that tomorrow he would call the Jury administrative office and persuade them to reschedule his service for another time.

Unfortunately, on the next day's phone call, the court officer said that as this is a Grand Jury for a murder trial, no exceptions would be made. Murray's neck muscles tightened, his eyes bulged, and his voice cracked ever so slightly. He had to figure out a way to postpone this. Murray called back and offered the court officer a free fitting and a discount on alterations, but to no avail.

Realizing that the date would not change, Murray focused instead on getting released from the commitment. He alternately dreamt of Ruthie and researched ways of avoiding jury duty. He thought about applying for a federal job but remembered that he had failed the civil service exam three times. He contemplated joining the military (imagine telling Uncle Seymour!) but discovered that orientation was scheduled the same week as jury duty.

Ruthie called to say how eager she was for this special week, cooing into the receiver, prompting Murray to grab a few fistfuls of hair from the sides of his head. Murray had one avenue left. He must get himself dismissed from serving on this jury.

Murray did some more research and found that many attorneys want jurors who can easily be persuaded one way or the other. Showing education, intelligence, and logical reasoning often makes a jury candidate less desirable to the attorney. Murray started to feel better already. He would demonstrate his intelligence and accomplishments during his upcoming interview with the defense attorney.

When the interview date arrived, Murray wasted no time burnishing his image. After mentioning that he had once considered becoming a lawyer given his family's extensive experience with suits and briefs, Murray told the attorney that he had studied a semester abroad at Nigeria Community College, and had founded the Queens Village, NY chapter of the Queens Village, NY Stitch and Cuff trade association.

"He's perfect," said the defense attorney.

Another clump of hair came out of Murray's head.

But all hope was not lost—yet. Murray still had an interview with the prosecuting attorney, who might be persuaded to disqualify him. Murray redoubled his research efforts and found that acting stubborn, as if you know everything, often resulted in dismissal; attorneys were reluctant to spend the time and effort needed to deal with difficult individuals. Murray would focus on two particular pieces of advice: question the legitimacy of the grand jury proceedings, and mention the old saying that "a good prosecutor could get a jury to indict a ham sandwich." And use the George Carlin approach and say that he would make a great juror because he could spot guilty people by looking at them.

Rehearsed and confident, with an image of Ruthie prancing through his mind, Murray met the prosecuting attorney. But the pressure of the moment caused him to get a little confused. He said, "A good prosecutor could get a bland jury to ignite a liverwurst sandwich," and "I would make a grand juror because I can stop an innocent person a mile away."

"He's perfect," said the prosecuting attorney.

Now, Murray was having trouble finding any more hair on his head to pluck. The image of Ruthie dimmed. He paced the floor, did more research, whimpered, and then concluded that perhaps with a sufficient amount of groveling, he might persuade the sitting judge to excuse him. He called the judge, begged, and pleaded for an interview; after a long silence, the judge said yes. Cartwheels ensued.

Friends advised Murray to tell the judge that he would be unable to remain impartial at a murder trial. Worse, he was not a confrontational person, and if in the minority, could easily cave in to pressure from the majority. Murray prepared well and for the third time would attempt to get himself dismissed.

The judge seemed to be an agreeable fellow, and Murray, hiding his desperation well, launched right in. "I am against all murders, so it will be difficult for me to remain impartial. I am avid reader of murder mysteries, and after every one, I always side with the victim. Also, I can be easily pressured by others. There was this time at work when I knew a zigzag stitch was required, but Uncle

Seymour and Uncle Leo both insisted that a straight stitch would suffice, and I changed my opinion."

"He's perfect," said the judge

Murray was devastated. He called Ruthie knowing (hoping?) she would understand. After explaining his predicament and offering several other weeks as vacation alternatives, he heard silence on the other end. "Ruthie? Ruthie are you there?"

For Murray, high hemming season never dragged on as long as this one did. As his jury assignment approached, he tried to think positively. The trial could be intriguing. His fellow jurors might be interesting people. It wasn't really working.

On the day he was to report for jury duty, Murray woke up, dressed carelessly, ate a bland breakfast, then trudged to the courthouse, head bowed, chin dipping to his chest, and shoulders slightly hunched, still stung by the opportunity with Ruthie that fate had snatched away from him.

After a ten-minute walk made twenty minutes by his lethargy, Murray arrived at the courthouse and read the note posted to the door.

"Due to a conflict in the judge's schedule, this trial will postponed indefinitely."

• • •

SECTION 2

LIFE IN THE FAST LANE, OR HOW I LEARNED TO STOP WORRYING AND LOVE MY PSYCHIATRIST.

From my humble origins in Queens Village, I burst into the corporate world, determined to rise to the top, only to find that I was claustrophobic and unable to get on a crowded elevator. Harvey Slotnick, a childhood friend of mine and now one of world's preeminent pescatarians, who carries a 172 average in the Thursday night senior men's bowling league, suggested I see his psychiatrist. The shrink didn't help much with my claustrophobia, but he did recommend several companies where the executive suite was located on the first floor.

G O I N G   U P ?

Put me in an enclosed space any smaller than the Roman Coliseum, and claustrophobia rears its ugly head. That was before I was treated by the preeminent psychiatrist Doctor Wolfgang Otto von Bleichroeder, world-renowned not only for his seminal research on the psychological effects of bullying on rats during their formative years, but also for curing Fielding Mellish of his nagging self-doubt. The doctor had a quiet way about him but inspired great confidence. Before long, I was comfortably boarding tiny planes, squeezing into crowded elevators, and inserting myself into jammed subway cars. There was no sign of the claustrophobic demon; Doctor B had exorcised it. I would look forward to tight situations, scoff at them, and pity those people around me who were visibly uneasy—I could spot them every time. I was tempted to hand out Wolfgang Otto's card, but I felt that he might be too pricey.

One day, I was late for a meeting. I sprinted toward the closing doors of a crowded elevator, getting in just in time. The elevator made a half-hearted attempt to rise, but gave up halfway between the ground and first floors. Just another test for which I was well prepared. Although the elevator car was large, there were so many people in it that everyone's personal space was being violated. I immediately noticed my heartbeat quicken, but

I brushed it off as the result of my dash to the elevator. A few drops of sweat appeared on my forehead and ran amok under my arms, but I also attributed this to my recent exertion. Everyone on the elevator seemed to be taking the situation lightheartedly. The fellow behind me, several inches taller than I, began telling inane jokes that everyone thought were funny. Each time he opened his mouth to crack another one, his damp breath, which didn't smell so good either, would collide with the hairs on the back of my neck and moisten them in the process. Handkerchief in hand, I wiped my neck dry several dozen times in succession, hoping he would get the message, but the stupidity didn't cease.

Reflected from the inside of the shiny, mirror-like, entombing elevator door, inches from my nose, was my face and the scene behind me. I noted both the laughing expressions of my fellow riders and the growing bulge in my eyeballs. My heart, normally reliable, went a few seconds without beating and then pounded furiously to make up for the work it just missed. I was thankful the closed elevator doors would serve as a barrier, preventing my ticker from flying out of my chest. No more than a few minutes could have passed when my salivary glands forgot about the importance of their role in bodily stasis and caused my throat, mouth, and tongue to become so arid that even sandpaper seemed temptingly moist. Perplexed as to why everyone but me was relaxed about our predicament, I tried to shift uneasily, but space constraints prevented that.

Sensing foam gathering at the corners of my mouth and that urinary bladder control was waning, I frantically dialed Doctor Bleichroeder. I received a voicemail saying that he was in therapy. I was unsure whether he was giving it or receiving it. I dialed eighty-nine more times during the next minute, expecting a different result but not getting one. I would have increased this rate to 109 per minute, but my cell phone overheated and shut down. I convinced the spittlebug behind me to lend me his phone and then dialed it four dozen times before finally getting through to the Wolfman. Although I anticipated some useful advice from him in time to forestall the generation of foam overcoming my ability to clear it, he instead asked me what I thought I should do in this situation.

Gathering myself after the unexpected bursting of several blood vessels in my right eye, I fumed at Doctor B, "I thought I should call you."

It struck me then, that after ten years and $65,000 worth of therapy, I had never heard the doctor say anything other than, "What do you think you should do?" and "Same time, next week?" even when I asked him to recommend a good Chinese restaurant in the neighborhood.

By now, the noise from my pounding heart was interfering with everyone's ability to hear the jokes being told, and the sweat patches under my arms had traveled down to my socks. What was I going to do? It occurred to me that I would think positive thoughts. Maybe I did receive some good advice from my therapist—no, now I remember, I read that in *Prevention* magazine, which if you subscribe for two years, will cost less than sixty cents an issue, a rate somewhat lower than I was paying Doctor B. After several deep breaths, I calmed myself enough to allow my brain to think constructively. My eyes darted to the two people on either side of me, and I wondered if I could eat them if we were still stuck in the elevator after our food supply ran out. Well, that was hardly useful. Then I remembered that, thankfully, I had trimmed my fingernails this morning and would avoid damaging the elevator doors or my fingers when I began trying to claw my way out. So much for positive thoughts, I decided. I will have to remember to cancel my subscription to Prevention once I get out of here.

All of the laughing and joke-telling was interrupted by the sound of periodic whimpering. Everybody heard it. Even I heard it, and we all wondered where it was coming from.

It was me.

I only vaguely remember our extrication. Rescue workers hacked through the elevator doors mere moments before our air supply ran out. Some of my fellow elevator captives kid me, saying that the elevator resumed working properly after four-and-a-half minutes, but I am certain that could not have been true.

Recovery was slow but steady. Within three months, my eyeballs retreated back into their sockets, and my stuttering diminished enough to allow me to order a cup of coffee in public. Intending to pay dear Doctor Bl-Bl- Bl-Bl-Bleichroeder a cordial visit, I gathered together my recent medical records, some pastries, and a baseball bat. When I arrived, I found that his office was boarded up. A kind fellow in the next building told me that the person who used to occupy the shuttered office was Razlan Nicolescu, a Romanian emigre, known in the neighborhood as a skilled carpenter, whose hobby was psychiatry.

• • •

THE JOY
OF TRAVELING

Business during the year 2004, which felt much longer than twelve months, had me crossing the Atlantic to the United States from my home in London fifteen times. Squeezed into that schedule were three trips to Japan, further increasing my frequent flier mileage balance and adding to an already unhealthy level of sleep debt. And so it was with a wan smile and some unintelligible murmuring that I greeted my wife's suggestion to gather up our four children, ages two through eleven, for a year-end vacation to Disney World in Florida.

With undue haste, my wife made our reservations, and we were now just a transatlantic flight (another one) away from jostling with thousands of people competing for the attention of a dozen Disney characters, and the privilege of waiting in line for irrationally long periods of time for a turn on various amusement park rides, lasting a couple of minutes each. The days turned into hours and the hours into minutes, or so it seemed, each day the same, and each evening marked by exhaustion—for the parents only.

I cannot deny that Disney entertains children, and, as always, I enjoyed watching my children have the time of their lives. I even secretly fancied some of the exhibits at Epcot and thought some of rides were thrilling—until we boarded our flight home to London. Following a short daytime flight from Orlando, we left Atlanta on a Sunday night. The accumulation of incessant air travel followed by a week of running after four young children had me bleary-eyed, fatigued, and sobbing involuntarily—but only occasionally. I settled into my window seat, thinking only of sleep. Minutes into the flight, my gentle doze was violently interrupted by the newsworthy announcement—made at a decibel level far exceeding OSHA safety limits—that this flight (like every other one for the past two decades) was non-smoking. Thanks. The Sandman again began to work his magic. Struggling to support the weight of my head and eyelids, I sleepily looked outside the airplane and saw a blue Samsonite suitcase, remarkably similar to the one I checked in, float by the window. Now, I knew just how tired I was; so tired that I was hallucinating.

Before long, I was again shaken from my sleep. Dinner was served. Partway through the meal, the flight attendant took the intercom and announced, "We have a minor technical problem. There is not enough oxygen being sent into the cabin. Do not be alarmed." What else does one become after a message like that? After a few more tries at saying something reassuring (she was unable to), the captain finally took over and said we were returning to Atlanta because the plane could not maintain cabin pressure above six thousand feet. Apparently, the seal on the cargo door didn't work properly, and the door was partially open. Well, that explained the suitcase I saw earlier.

We returned to Atlanta, where the captain informed us we were not allowed to deplane because of some arcane customs rule, and that the maintenance crew would work on the plane at the gate. He explained that after the plane was fixed, they would have to test the pressurization of the cabin. During such a test, the doors could not be opened, and if something were to happen—

such as a fire— none of us would be able to get out. He wisely reconsidered his position on the custom rules and instructed us to leave the aircraft. The airline offered passengers the option to stay the night in Atlanta, or to wait for the aircraft to be made airworthy. As you might imagine, it was rather difficult to warm up to that particular plane, so we chose to stay in Atlanta.

On Monday night, we shoved off again for London, and on this plane, the cargo door sealed itself like a charm. With only twenty minutes of the flight remaining, the plane was struck by lightning. This pleasurable experience included a loud explosion, a bright purplish flash of light, the rocking of the aircraft, and the flight attendant nearest to me shrieking, "Oh my God!" with her once well-coiffed hair now standing straight up. It sounded to me as if the engines had blown up. I was unconcerned knowing I had my seatbelt fastened. Not a word from the cockpit, then or during the rest of the flight. It probably took at least that long for the pilot to climb out from under his seat and cease his trembling.

Obviously, we landed successfully. As we were deplaning, we overheard one of the pilots animatedly discussing the incident with ground personnel, suggesting that perhaps it wasn't a run-of-the-mill experience. Sure glad I don't have to get on another plane for almost a full two weeks.

• • •

THE GANG THAT COULDN'T SHOOT STRAIGHT

They told me on a Friday afternoon, the day before the start of my two-week vacation. When I returned, I would begin working for the European Division of the multinational company that employed me. A transfer to the European Division ranked last in financial performance among all the divisions in the company, was known within the company as the graveyard shift.

Only it wasn't a shift; it was a three-year assignment. A more suitable description would be the professional equivalent of an elephant graveyard, where careers, instead of elephants, went to die.

The division consisted of fourteen countries, each managed by a seasoned professional of the same nationality. Rounding out the management team were the supervisor of human resources, a British woman so stubborn in her views that she made Margaret Thatcher seem wishy-washy, and me, the lone American, in charge of finance. We all reported to a Swiss-German gentleman, Gunter Blatter, the living embodiment of the Peter Principle, whose social development had sputtered and died sometime around the second grade.

Come to think of it, his cerebral development probably peaked around the same time. Herr Blatter bore a remarkable resemblance—both physically and intellectually—to Sergeant Schultz of *Hogan's Heroes*. His thoughts, when he had them, were black and white, nuance as alien to him as showing warmth to a fellow human being.

Tell him a joke or a humorous story, and his eyes would hollow out while his eyelids froze, signaling to the jokester that Blatter's brain neurons had called one of its customary—and lengthy—time outs.

How he came to be division head of this very large multinational corporation competes with the Bermuda Triangle as one of the world's great unsolved mysteries. I wasn't clear about whether Mr. Blatter recognized that each of us felt we must have committed heinous crimes in our previous lives to find ourselves, in this one, as subordinates of his. In his own uncluttered mind, he may have believed he deserved to be boss.

Anyway, here we all were, the European Division managers, ready to be led to greatness or at least to meeting our budget goals. We were an unruly, disparate bunch, and it didn't help that each member of the team carried with them ancient historical and cultural grudges, some of them at least one thousand years old. Gunter did know how to start and end a meeting on time; however, we actively conspired to negate even those elementary skills.

If the willingness of a group of professionals to run through a wall at the boss's command is the hallmark of a highly motivated team working for a capable, well-liked, and respected leader, then our dogged hunt for a door was a referendum on Gunter Blatter's effectiveness.

A typical management meeting, held once a month, conducted in English—although that wasn't always apparent—began with the French Country Head, Claude Lambert, arriving fifteen minutes late and setting the tone for the rest of the day. Punctuality was sacred to Herr Blatter, a fact that was well known to Claude, who never missed an opportunity to desecrate. A red spot would appear on Blatter's neck, and, like injected dye, would travel upward until it engulfed his entire face.

Blatter, who had trouble thinking clearly in the best of times, lost control of both mind and speech—and the meeting. This was when we polished up on our German curse words. Claude would smile throughout, as if to remind Blatter who was on the losing end of the two world wars, but also to convey to the boss how unlikely it was that he, Claude, would do anything that Blatter directed him to do. Flummoxed, and determined to get the session back on track, Blatter repeated, for a fourth time, the agenda and goals for the meeting and read some passages from *Mein Kampf*.

The first manager scheduled to present his financial performance was the Italy Country Head, Aldo Mandolini. At five foot five inches, Aldo was small in physical stature, and small in intellectual stature as well. He gave the impression that he did not know what he was doing or managing, and did so convincingly. Unlike the stereotypical suave, debonair Italian, Aldo's hair begged for a comb, his suit for an iron, and his breath for a mint.

He always seemed to have just come in from a rainstorm or a tussle with one of his paramours—and that was what he looked like at the start of the meeting. Aldo spoke so quickly and with such a pronounced stammer that no one really knew what he was saying, although it was the considered view of most people in the room that it probably wouldn't be any different if he spoke slowly without stammering. While speaking, Aldo had a habit of reflexively looking to his right and to his left, probably a vestige of his military days when he was trained to be alert to the signs of a retreating army.

Next up was the Greece Country Head, Stavros Antonopoulos. We all believed that Stav's wheeling and dealing with his fellow countrymen in the shipping industry (on company time) was earning him far more than the compensation from our company. Throughout the entire meeting, he had a cellphone glued to his ear, gripped tightly by fingers yellowed by the overuse of filterless Camels. When called upon by Blatter, he shrugged while pointing to his cell phone, and he left the room, intending to project a sense of courtesy to the rest of us, which no one ever bought. Blatter's eye twitch usually worsened. Only when we were onto a new topic would Stav reappear in the conference room, invariably cursing the Turks under his breath for causing his absence. No one bought that either.

One of the chairs at the conference table, for the Sweden Country Head, Lars Dahlberg, was always empty. I wondered why until I read that "Swedish parental leave . . . provides 480 days of leave per child. Sixty days of the paid leave are reserved for each parent, and the remaining joint allowance can be divided between the mother and father as they choose."

Over the last six years, Lars's wife, Astrid, had blessed Lars with five healthy children, each one coming about a year and two months apart. Astrid, who enjoyed working, took her required sixty days, leaving the 420-day balance to her husband. No one at our company had seen Lars in more than a half-decade, during which time our company's business in Sweden had shrunk by nearly two-thirds.

Coincidentally, a friend of mine at one of our competitors mentioned that he also worked with a fellow named Lars Dahlberg who also had a wife named Astrid and five children. My friend said they never saw Lars at his company either. Lars had perfected the art of Extraknäck.

Willy Mertens, the Belgium Country Head, an affable, overweight fellow, kept us all entertained without realizing it. A knowledgeable businessman, Willy could always be counted on for incisive business analysis whenever he was sober and awake. Unlike Claude Lambert, Willy was reliably punctual, being sure to deposit his oversized frame, bloodshot eyes, and drooping eyelids into his favorite chair at the conference table, no later than thirty minutes before the meeting started, a useful time to socialize.

However, Willy preferred to use that half-hour to count sheep. Several times during the meeting, Willy would lumber to the rear of the room, where a coffee urn and a table of pastries were set up. There, Willy would surreptitiously—or so he thought—remove a flask from his inner suit pocket and pour generously into his coffee cup. He returned to his seat convinced that no one in the room was aware of, or had ever seen, the flask. However, we all knew that it was three-inches high, made of polished silver, sported a stylish leather covering on the bottom, and had Willy's initials engraved on the side in Arial Black font.

Our business in Spain was managed by the garrulous and restless Juan Carlos Huertas. JC held no grudges, save one; he couldn't help sneering down his long Castilian nose at our

Portugal Country Head, Joao Pinheiro, and for good reason. Pinheiro had been caught on more than one occasion attempting to lace the Spaniard's coffee with a powder reputed to induce diarrhea. Neither Huertas nor Pinheiro have quite gotten over the Portuguese War for Independence in 1640 and were still miffed about a couple of the provisions of the Treaty of Lisbon, which granted Portugal its independence in 1668.

Gunter Blatter knew that the completion of the meetings' agenda would be in jeopardy once Huertas got going, yet he was powerless to stop the Spaniard. Huertas pontificated on every topic raised, always sounded intelligent, and went unchallenged because all of us were happy to continue completing our Sudoku grids while he held the floor. I figured that Juan Carlos could trace his lineage back to one of the great Greek or Roman orators.

He fidgeted while seated as others were speaking, but, when it was his turn, he vaulted out of his chair like a man freed from prison after a decade of splitting stones with a pickax. Huertas never spoke; he declaimed. And for that, he must be on his feet, pacing around the meeting room to make a point or answer a question, even if asked whether he preferred tuna fish salad or ham and cheese for lunch. Huertas would circle the conference table, head bowed, lips in motion, pacing behind the chairs in which we sat.

You knew he was getting close to you by the waft of garlic on his breath. Every few steps, he would stop, look up and place his hands on the shoulders of the person seated in the chair at which he'd stopped so that he could properly emphasize the point he was making. "I'll have the tuna." By the time he finished his soliloquy, everyone had been touched except Mr. Pinheiro. After a couple of meetings, this began to seem creepy. The next time Juan Carlos began his peregrination, two of the country heads excused themselves and darted to the men's room. Then two more did the same. By the meeting's end, the Spaniard was talking to an empty conference room, all of us— except Gunter and his shoulders— being either in the men's room or outside the building grabbing a cigarette, even those who didn't smoke.

Last to speak was the England Country head, Duncan Clarke-Cooper, our own Ralph Nettleby from The Shooting Party, who had us believing that he was pure British aristocracy. But, although he strutted, tut-tutted, and dabbed only the side of his mouth with his napkin, I suspected he might be a closet hooligan.

He did little to hide his impatience with these management meetings and with the human beings in attendance, particularly ones from the insufferable countries of Europe and a former colony across the Atlantic. He sat motionless at the meetings, jacket always on and sporting a stiff upper lip, which we could always use to open the San Pellegrino we had with lunch. If nothing else, Duncan Clarke-Cooper was fair—he annoyed everyone. I couldn't pinpoint whether he was born that way or just worked very hard at it. As he settled into his chair at the beginning of each meeting, Duncan would conspicuously place a biography of Winston Churchill, a different book each meeting, as an unsubtle reminder to Blatter about who won the last world war. Gunter pretended not to notice, but his eye twitch gave him away.

However, Duncan reserved his sharpest needle for Claude Lambert. As a self-proclaimed student of history, Duncan would pepper his conversation with quotes such as "I would rather have a German division in front of me than a French one behind me" (General George S. Patton) or "The best thing I know between France and England is the sea" (Douglas William Jerrold). All the while, Claude would remain outwardly unflappable—smiling, arms extended on the table, hands clasped, with his cufflinks bearing the number "1066" in plain view—while inwardly wishing to thrash Duncan with a baguette.

Every European management meeting was a real-life version of *Groundhog Day*. They were remarkably effective at preserving both ancient rivalries and the downward financial trajectory of the business. The only thing that could possibly have helped would have been a miracle— or the promotion up and out of Gunter Blatter.

• • •

JET LAG

Japan is known as the "Land of the Rising Sun," reflecting the belief held by ancient Japanese that their islands were the first land in the world awakened by the rising sun. I frequently traveled from New York to Japan on business. Each time, I fell asleep as the sun was rising and woke up well after it set. This did little to enhance my career because my boss, a traditionalist, conducted business meetings during the day and expected everyone to maintain consciousness throughout.

It all started with a flight that lasted fourteen hours and, seemingly passed through an equal number of time zones. Unlike some of my naturally melatonin-rich colleagues who step off long flights with their circadian rhythms intact, I deplane with the cerebral equivalent of cotton mouth. Knowing this, I plan a strict regimen on the flight: a full meal including one glass of wine, followed by one movie to induce me into seven to eight hours of sleep—only it never works. But on this flight, I tried again. After meal, wine, and movie, in went the earplugs, and on went the sleep mask, and for thirty minutes, nothing happened. So, with another glass of wine, I washed down a large snack and watched a second movie. Still nothing. By now, seven hours into the flight, everyone else on the plane was asleep. Being the only one awake, I was also the only one concerned by the sound of snoring coming from both chairs in the cockpit. I stood to stretch my legs, walked to the serving area, and gently woke the flight attendant to request another glass of wine. I watched a third movie, read seventy-five pages of *Non-Linear and Asymptotic Systems and Signals*, and still no sign of the Sandman.

After thirteen and one-half hours of flying, the captain, thankfully awake after a good night's sleep, announced that we were preparing for descent into Narita Airport. This coincided with my own descent into a time-zone-induced, coma-like sleep. With the plane landed and now empty, the flight attendant, having failed to awaken me, called the maintenance crew, who unbolted the seat from the aisle and took me off the plane.

I struggled to remain upright and awake in the queues for customs and immigration. The fellow in front of me disgustedly swatted away my head as it attempted to come to rest on his shoulder. Eventually, the fellow gave up, and so together, Siamese twin–like, we trudged through the long line. I did my best not to snore too loudly in his ear or drool in excess on his shirt.

Finished with customs, I gathered my luggage, hailed a taxi, and headed directly to the first of several meetings scheduled that day. These meetings, a series of presentations held in a conference room, were straightforward, routine, and boring to those with a full night's sleep, deadening to victims of sleeplessness and jet lag.

About five minutes into the first meeting, the passage of time slowed considerably; I heard only every other word spoken by the presenter. If I was meant to be contributing to the meeting, I wasn't. The effort to create any sound resembling a word was too daunting. After ten minutes, I was lucky to register one word per sentence as I lost control of my head and eyelids. *I'll just close my eyes for a moment.* The relief was profound. To my horror, when I reopened them, what I thought was a few seconds later, a different person was presenting, and a small pool of saliva had accumulated on my tie. How many people had noticed? Did it look as bad as I was imagining? A lot, and yes. Spotting a coffee urn in the back of the room, I served myself a cup and returned to my seat. The speaker's lips were moving, but nothing audible was coming out; I was drifting off again. I willed myself awake and went back for another cup of coffee.

Hoping that a splash of water on my face would be helpful, I headed to the men's room. A few handfuls of water on my face didn't really do anything, so I placed my head in the sink under the running faucet. My brain, again fooled, that the horizontal position of my head meant a pillow had appeared, sent signals to my eyelids to close and for rapid eye movement to begin. Based on how soggy my shirt, tie, and upper part of my pants were, I guessed that I had been asleep for thirty minutes. I couldn't return to the conference room soaking wet, so I crouched under the hand dryer and taped the on button down so it wouldn't stop. Mistaking the flow of soothing, warm air for the tranquilizing feeling of lying snuggly under a comforter, my easily fooled brain sent instructions to skip rapid eye movement and go directly to stage three slow eye movement (the stage that precedes coma). After some noises coming from patrons of the men's room woke me, I sprinted to the conference room to find it empty, which also aptly described my prospects for career advancement.

I still had dinner to get through. Relief—pillow and bed—were only about two hours away. But to save my job, I had to demonstrate I was still capable of thinking and speaking. Food and wine, which had failed badly to produce sleep on the airplane, were remarkably effective at the restaurant. With my eyelids drooping and my job on the line, the toothpicks in the hors d'oeuvres looked more tempting than the hors d'oeuvres. Dinner progressed. I grew sleepier, but as long as I was drinking or chewing, I was less likely to fall asleep in my soup or entree. My mouth in full chew, I turned to converse with the gentleman to my left. My addled brain fixed on his pale complexion, round face, and starched white shirt, convincing my eyes that I was seated next to a talking pillow. Well, that was hardly what I needed, so I turned to chat with the lady on my right. Her short, straight, light brown, Edna Mode–style haircut sat atop her head like the shade on my night table lamp at home . . . next to my bed . . . where I sleep.

Somehow, I made it to the end of dinner, never having had a conversation with anyone and avoiding dozing off by continual, excessive eating. I left the restaurant, scurried back to the hotel, and headed straight to bed for that long, deep sleep I had craved all day. Tomorrow, I would be refreshed and alert for the next day's vapid presentations. I set the alarm for 7:00 a.m., tumbled into bed, and yielded to the Greek god, Hypnos. He never arrived. Instead of shutting my system down, my dysfunctional body clock switched into high gear. Lying in bed was pointless, so I sat up and read, watched TV, ate, read some more, and watched more TV until the alarm went off propelling me into a real-life version of the movie *Groundhog Day*.

• • •

HOTEL
CALIFORNIA

Last month, I believe I set the record for the longest hospital stay for a medical procedure without complications. Guys who checked in after me left with different hearts than the one they came in with and wished me a speedy recovery on their way out. My doctor put the "ultra" in ultra-conservative, and he seemed to have a keen interest in learning just how long a human being could remain attached to an intravenous drip. So lengthy was my stay that I began to have positive feelings toward my captor, er, doctor. I also fell in love with my IV walker. After all, we went everywhere together; we even slept together—and I affectionately named it Ivy.

My ordeal began at home when an ulcer decided to pierce a part of my duodenum, which happened to be adjacent to a major vein. I don't know how long this ulcer was beavering away at the vein, but the breakthrough occurred on a Saturday afternoon when I was relieving myself in the bathroom. Suddenly, the hard, cold, tiled floor looked like a very attractive place to rest my head. I remember successfully easing my head to the floor, although my family members, who heard a loud thud reverberating throughout the house, seem to think differently.

When I came to, I was lying on the floor, surrounded by a half-dozen people and attached to so many IVs, that had they been balloons, I would have floated toward the ceiling. My son kept telling me, "Stay with us," which I found an odd request because I didn't feel much like going anywhere, and I had decided earlier in the day to give away my tickets to the Puerto Rico Symphony's performance that evening.

Soon enough, I arrived at the hospital, where they placed a tube through my nose into my stomach, and then one into my rear end, which felt like it also reached my stomach. Or was it the rear end tube that went in first and the nose tube second? Or maybe they were both inserted at the same time. That part was a little blurry, but whatever happened, I do remember ricocheting off the ceiling, returning to the bed with the nose tube in my rear end, and the rear-end tube in my nose. The alert doctor quickly corrected this and may have even cleaned each tube off before reinsertion, but I was too groggy to notice. A few hundred radiation-laden tests later—X-rays, MRIs, CAT scans, electrocardiograms—and I was delivered, slightly aglow, to my prison cell hospital room.

I am not paranoid like those guys who are always hearing voices in their heads; I hear them only occasionally. My unease grew when everybody assigned to my care—and I mean everybody: nurses, nurses-in-training, doctors, doctors-in-training—would look everywhere but into my eyes and say that I had the most conservative doctor in Puerto Rico. No one was willing to explain what they meant by "conservative." I brushed that off and focused on my condition: a dangerously low hemoglobin level of 8.2g, which I had to build back up to my normal level of 15g. How unusual, then, that every morning (why did they have to do this at 4:30 a.m.?) the nurse—Nurse Ratched, I think her name was—would take from me what I needed most: a blood sample and some of my precious hemoglobin. Each night, my doctor would visit, gravely informing me that my hemoglobin level was not going up.

Well. I considered discussing my theory with him but feared that he might instruct the nurse to increase the size of the daily blood sample to keep me docile.

A day or two into my stay, I thought I overheard one of the nurses mention that my doctor had a substantial financial interest in a company that supplied the hospital with hypodermic needles, a plausible explanation for my treatment as a pin cushion. At least four times a day, some sort of needle penetrated my skin. My favorites were the daily, deep intramuscular injections of vitamin K and iron. I would bend over, hold onto a wooden chair in front of me for support, and the nurse would sink two impossibly long needles, one into each buttock. In her zeal to get the deep part right, the nurse would often have to dislodge the needle tip from the wooden chair I was holding onto. I have seen so many stars that I now have all the constellations memorized.

If four needles a day were not enough, after a week, a new nurse suddenly appeared two days in a row to prick my finger (with a needle, of course) testing for glucose. No one had explained to me why glucose is a concern to someone with an inadequate supply of hemoglobin—which, of course, it isn't. The nurse returned to my room to say "Whoops!" and told me that the glucose test was meant for the fellow in the room next to mine.

Either Doc just wanted to sell two more needles, or he was fishing for a bad glucose reading to keep me "under observation" for a few more days, or both. When he told me that one night that week he would be unable to check in on me and would send another doctor in his place, I presumed it was because his attendance was required at the National Needle, Syringe, and Intravenous Fluid Association's Gala Dinner, where he would be the honored guest.

I concluded that being on the receiving end of an error at a hospital—a rare event—placed me in a select group. Perhaps I would be interviewed for a scholarly article in the *Journal of Medicine*. I figured that it would be years before this institution made its next mistake, that is, until the night nurse told me that I had been scheduled for ACL surgery the next morning.

The days turned into weeks. The formula for my captivity—keep me too weak to leave the hospital—was simple. Take daily blood samples, withdrawing all the recuperative hemoglobin my body was generating, and feed me liquids only. It was working well until one day my hemoglobin shot up by 1g, from 8.4g to 9.4g, a remarkable increase in a single day. Doc was clearly not happy about this stunning improvement and wasted no time putting Nurse Ratched to work. Next morning's blood sample took a lot longer than usual, reminiscent of the eighteenth century's state-of-the-art medical practice of bloodletting. It worked (for Doc) as my hemoglobin returned to the 8.4 g level.

Say what you want about Doc, but he was a delightful conversationalist with a warm bedside manner. After several days of IV fluids only, fearful that the muscles enabling me to chew and swallow were becoming vestigial like the wings on the flightless ostrich, I asked the doctor if my wife could bring me a nutritious drink. "Not unless you want Nurse Ratched to take two samples per day," came the warm response.

Because he made his hospital rounds in the evening, my wife snuck in some apple juice one morning, my first ingestion of a liquid in what seemed an eternity. I savored it, kept it on a table near me, and drank it slowly so that it would last me as much of the day as possible. Without warning, the doctor appeared, conducting his rounds in the afternoon this one and only day. Was tonight the Needle and Syringe Association's dinner? Oh no—the open apple juice!

My pulse quickened, my saliva vanished, my sweat poured, my eyelids twitched. I was surely in for another round of bloodletting if the doctor spotted the forbidden juice. I lurched forward from my seat, intending to use my body to obstruct the doctor's view of the apple juice, but stumbled over my IV caddy, nearly ripping the IV needle from my arm, giving me another view of those pretty constellations. Good fortune arrived in the form of the nurse, two hypodermic needles in her holster, looking for any unbroken skin on my buttocks to penetrate. The doctor temporarily excused himself, allowing me to quaff the remaining juice and dispose of the evidence. I never enjoyed a deep intramuscular injection as much as I did just then.

To this day, I am not quite sure how I ever got out of the hospital, although on the day I departed, my wife dressed me in a fedora and raincoat and told me to sprint to the elevators. I am now living comfortably, somewhere, with a new name under the Witness Protection Program.

I miss Ivy.

• • •

NATIONAL SERVICE
FOR ALL

Many U.S. presidents have supported the idea of mandatory national service. President John F. Kennedy did so most eloquently, saying, "Ask not what your country can do for you; ask what you can do for your country." He considered such work ennobling, giving Americans a chance to "share a common civic experience rooted in the ideals of commitment and sacrifice." For these reasons and many more, I also think every American should work, for a period of time, for the government. So much can be learned, making for better-informed citizens and voters.

During my two years of work at the Defense Department, my boss, Mr. McKenna, taught me the importance of getting sufficient sleep. Mr. McKenna wasn't one of those pretentious fellows who merely "talked the talk." My boss would "walk the walk" for all to see. After a quick lunch eaten at his desk at 11:30 a.m., Mac would take out a pillow and blanket from the bottom draw and sleep contentedly in his cubicle through much of the afternoon. Noises didn't seem to bother him, but then again, there wasn't much noise on the floor because there was hardly any work taking place. Not once, did I ever see Mr. McKenna tired at a meeting— underscoring his message about getting sufficient slumber—although I never did see any meetings either.

Every year, the Defense Department hired two college graduates. In 1974, it was a fellow named Brian and me—to keep the pipeline going. It hadn't occurred to the guys in charge that the pipeline had been leaking for quite some time because the ages of everyone else in the department were between sixty and one hundred. The primary responsibility of our office (which employed about two hundred employees with no more than twelve needed and not many more than that showing up) was to administer contracts between the Defense Department and the local aerospace industry. Whenever a contractor missed a milestone, the Defense Department amended the contract in exchange for consideration, a process that consumed about fifteen minutes. On a typical day, there were approximately ten such amendments to be spread among two hundred employees. Work at our office proceeded at a glacial pace, an affront to the dynamism of glaciers, crushing the spirit and ambition of any twenty-something-year-old naive enough to have wandered into its employ.

I figured this out in five days, while Brian, a particularly quick study, knew in four. Also much faster than anyone else, Brian grasped the import of Mr. McKenna's exhortations about frequent visits to the Sandman. It was in this regard that national service taught me a second significant lesson: the value of loyalty and teamwork.

For Brian, every night was a Friday or Saturday. He arrived at work each morning with glazed eyes, the victims of either too much alcohol, too little sleep, or both, sporting a variety of bloodshot reds matched only by Revlon's Fire And Ice lipstick. Brian carried with him a sleep debt that had to be repaid. Clever man that he was, Brian noticed that the toilet paper dispenser in the stalls in the men's room was a simple device, affixed to the wall at a level slightly higher than the seat, without any covering, fluffy toilet paper exposed, measuring a precise torso length from the toilet—

almost as if he designed it himself. At first, Brian would spend only an hour or so in the stall, sleeping with his head comfortably nestled on the strategically located toilet paper, the best pillow in the office, save McKenna's. Being a reliable colleague, I promised to go get him if any of the managers questioned where he was. No one ever wondered, though, so Brian slept longer, so long, that the only thing anybody wondered about was whether Brian still worked there.

Well, a day came when the bosses were looking for Brian, and by then, even I was unsure whether he worked there any longer. While some of the executives started milling about impatiently, I sprinted to the men's room and banged on every stall door, doing my best imitation of Paul Revere to alert Brian to the gathering storm. Not wishing for the bosses to see me walking into the office with Brian, I took a different route back inside and stood behind them as Brian emerged, the toilet paper perforations freshly imprinted on his forehead. Worse, a fragment of toilet paper dangled from his cheek. As Brian entered the room to confront the phalanx of bigwigs, he should have seen behind them, a head (mine) periodically bobbing above theirs, using facial signals, unsuccessfully, to warn him of his unique appearance. After administering a stern warning, the overlords went back to doing nothing in the days that followed, and Brian resumed his lengthy bathroom visits. For my part, I discovered that Brian was still an employee, and therefore needed my help as loyal watchdog.

Which brings me to the third important lesson learned from my time in government service: punctuality. Our workday began at 8:30 a.m. and ended at 4:30 p.m.—not 4:31 p.m. or 4:32

p.m.—but 4:30 p.m. Although the day ended at 4:30 p.m., "work" ceased at 4:00 p.m., because all of the employees—even Brian left the stalls no later than 4:00 p.m.—gathered their belongings, put on their hats and coats if it were winter, and sat motionless, like the calcified Politburo of the former Soviet Union, craning their necks to focus on the minute hand of the wall clock. Banter was not permitted because we were, of course, still within "working" hours. When that magical moment arrived, even Pamplona's bulls would have marveled at the stampede that ensued. Women jostled as aggressively as the men, chivalry suspended, as two hundred people fought to leave the building before the minute hand could finish a turn around the clock. Never before or since, have I seen such a coordinated display of punctuality from so large a group. And if you think it was a fluke, it wasn't. It was orchestrated with the same degree of precision, every day.

By 8:45 a.m. each day, I, like most everyone in the office, had completed my assigned work, leaving a rather large chunk of time to fill. Being young and ambitious, I hunted for reading material to enhance my knowledge and skills. I began perusing Defense Department Procurement Manuals, a natural soporific made even more powerful by the sound of McKenna snoring. My eyes closed. After my head involuntarily bounced off my metal desk for the second time, I realized that it was inadvisable to continue. So, I did nothing, watching the clock in anticipation of lunch hour, but that too caused my head to take a beating from the metal desk. Not everyone had the same problem. Many of my colleagues were busy—just not on government work. Most of the dedicated public servants in the office were double-dippers who openly conducted their personal real estate, attorney, appraisal businesses at their desks, but only after their Defense Department work was completed, which pretty much left the whole day. At the time, I was attending MBA graduate school at night. Feeling emboldened, I furtively read a few pages of my course textbook at my desk; a then, a chapter; and then, two. Before long, all my MBA materials covered my desk as I prepared homework, studied for exams, and wrote my thesis. Who was going to notice? McKenna? I did surprisingly well in grad school, thanks in large part to my employment at the Defense Department.

All in all, my government service was an excellent learning experience, an experience I think everyone should have, and would, if national service were mandatory.

.

• • •

THANKS FOR THE MEMORIES

With increasing frequency, my wife's memory was losing its sharpness. Although more bothersome than serious, her forgetfulness was not something that either of us was willing to overlook. We searched high and low for potential remedies and cures but without much success. She tried mental exercises, Sudoku puzzles, diets rich in "brain food." Almost by chance, we stumbled onto an exciting alternative medicine we felt, after reading the label, was precisely what we needed.

Triple-Strength Memory Enhancer

Recommended Dosage: Take one a day, always with food since it can be harsh on the stomach. Take an additional two tablets if any of the following situations occur:

1. You forget where you left your keys.
2. You remember that your husband's name begins with R, but are unsure of the rest.
3. You forget where you left your cellphone.
4. On the way out of the house to drive your daughter to school, your husband kisses you goodbye and hands you your cellphone. After getting into the car, you "remember" that you don't have your cell phone and return to the house to get it.
5. You forget where you left your sneakers.

6. You leave the house on a trip to Aguadilla and return home to retrieve your cellphone. You leave a second time and return again to retrieve your purse. You leave a third time, but by now, it is so late in the day that no one is at home to record the number of additional times you returned to the house.

7. You wake up in the middle of the night and have no clue who is sleeping next to you.

8. You wake up in the middle of the night, have no clue who is sleeping next to you, and grab a pair of scissors for defensive purposes.

9. You wake up in the middle of the night, have no clue who is sleeping next to you, and grab a pair of scissors for offensive purposes. Should this happen, swallow all the remaining pills in the bottle at once. No need to eat food with them. Your stomach will be just fine; in fact, you may chew the pills if you cannot find water to wash them down. If this dosage hasn't worked, leave the house at once, and do not forget to take the scissors, particularly if blood-stained, with you for proper disposal. Change your identity.

• • •

MISOPHONIACS UNITE!

The impact of this little-known, debilitating illness (misophonia, or selective sound sensitivity syndrome) on thousands of long-suffering victims goes unnoticed and unappreciated every day. Literature, clinics, and support groups are nonexistent. If we're lucky, we suffer in silence. More than likely, we are ridiculed. In fact, the only sympathy I ever receive after an attack of misophonia is from my wife, who is concerned enough to ask me, "What the hell is the matter with you?" although she never waits around for me to answer.

Put me in an agreeable social situation—lots of friendly people, good food, lively music, interesting conversation—and I will hear, and then fixate on the dog barking in the distance. Can I help it if I have the auricular sensitivity of, well, a dog?

I might be trying to close an important business deal over lunch in a restaurant when my attention is stolen by the person at a nearby table, sniffling and snorting, never having been taught (or perhaps having forgotten), how effective a tissue or handkerchief can be in such situations. In an attempt to alert the sniffler to his churlish behavior, I sniffle and snort, only louder. This invariably leads my lunch guest to ask the same question my wife does.

When I occasionally fly first class, I eagerly look forward to a quiet meal. Instead, I am assaulted by the cacophony of knives and forks striking china as diners sloppily cut and spear their food. Just how difficult is it to target one's food noiselessly? All at once, my taste buds, hunger, and equanimity shut down. With each clanging fork and knife, my rage deepens.

Even at home in Puerto Rico, the endemic coqui, a small frog less than one-inch long, emits a delightful mating call, part of the music of the tropics. For months, I enjoyed the soothing sounds until a mutant coqui with the lungs of Enrico Caruso settled into one of the plants in our outdoor terrace. Clearly, this was one sex-deprived coqui, its mutation having frightened off a number of eligible female coquis. Its mating calls were louder, more frequent, and more desperate than any I had heard before. Eating dinner, watching TV, conversing with the family became impossible. As soon as I entered the terrace, the coqui would clam up, so I couldn't identify in which plant he was perched. I hosed down the entire terrace, poured scalding hot water into each of the plants, and then tried citric acid. Nothing worked. Napalm or Agent Orange seemed to be the logical next steps, but I had trouble convincing my wife.

I first became aware of my affliction as a youngster, when after dinner, our family would settle into the living room and my dad's tongue would go in search of food particles that had decided to nestle in the spaces between his teeth rather than follow the intended path to his stomach.

The art of coaxing food out of its dental hiding place required that a suction be created between tongue and tooth, followed by the tongue's rapid release. This sometimes drew out the food but always produced a clicking sound. To the rest of the family, the click went unnoticed; to me, it sounded like a firecracker exploding in my face.

Our family of five lived in a tiny apartment of four rooms

separated by walls through which light and sound traveled freely. Trying to escape the click, I would take my books and homework first into the dining room, and then to the bedroom I shared with my brother (who made his own noises).

Invariably I ended up in the bathroom, which was a couple of extra feet away from the living room. No matter how hard I tried to concentrate on my schoolwork, I would, instead, be anticipating the next explosive click. My dad's tongue would methodically visit each tooth. My sanity precariously rested on his having had four wisdom teeth removed during his adolescence. The prospect that he could have been doing this thirty-two times a night instead of twenty-eight was unnerving. Eventually, the noise stopped, marking the completion of my dad's virtual flossing, a signal that I could leave the bathroom and rejoin the family. They never said anything to me, but they did look at me like I was nuts.

It never got any easier as the years passed. Commonplace sounds—sniffling, slurping, snoring, dogs barking, cutlery banging—would taunt and torment . . . every day. Because sympathy from loved ones was not forthcoming, I turned to man's best friend, but had to drop that idea when his barking set off an acute attack of misophonia.

When I moved my family to Puerto Rico, we chose what appeared to be a peaceful neighborhood, and it was—until Rocky moved in a few houses away. Rocky, a confused dog, thinking he was a rooster, not only announced the appearance of the new day's sun, but seemed intent on announcing its setting as well.

Being a dog and not a rooster, unequipped with any natural sense of when dusk would arrive, he would simply bark until it did. At first, all of the misophoniac's rage was directed at the rooster dog, but after much violent twitching and frothing, the sound-challenged victim recognized that the dog owner's lack of consideration, or his deafness, was to blame.

So, I had to confront Rocky's owner (Gilbert) but wisely decided to do so via text, rather than in person, because I wasn't at all sure I would be able to release my hands from his throat in a timely manner. So that others may learn more about, and come to appreciate, the misophoniac's plight, I have transcribed our text exchange, annotated with some explanatory comments.

<u>August 15, 7:04 a.m.</u>

Gilbert: I am Anita's husband. She received a note from you today regarding Rocky. I am in the States now and will be back Wednesday. She has been out of town and the kids, well, they are kids. *[Irresponsible of you to leave your kids alone like this.]* No one had charged his electric dog collar since I left almost a month ago. *[Why didn't Anita charge it? I presume Anita is not a kid since that would be a different kind of problem.]* Hopefully she will charge the collar tonight and get it back on Rocky tomorrow. The collar seems to work pretty well when it is charged! I apologize for the barking. It makes me crazy also. *[Also? So you think I am crazy? Just another example of the lack of understanding and ridicule heaped upon misophoniacs.]* Feel free to text or call me anytime.

August 15, 7:24 a.m.

Me: Thank you so much for your understanding. I spoke to Anita several months ago and was grateful for whatever she did. I didn't know there was such a thing as a barking collar *[I immediately purchased huge quantities at retail and offered them on eBay at a steep discount to encourage their use.]* because I haven't heard the dog barking until recently. I'll pay for the batteries and/or electricity to keep the collar charged. *[I also offer to teach your kids how to obey their parents and follow instructions.]*

August 16, 8:22 a.m.

Gilbert: Thanks, I bought it a couple of years ago when you first sent a note *[See! I have been working at this for two YEARS now. The world simply doesn't care about people who have this affliction.]* While our house was under construction, we slept in a bedroom right next to Rocky, and I got to hear him. Anita charged the collar last night and hopefully put it back on him this morning. I'll be home Wednesday to double check that it is set correctly. *[Gee Gil, we are not performing heart surgery here.]* Thanks for your cooperation.

September 6, 7:08 a.m.

Me: Unfortunately the dog collar doesn't appear to be working at all this morning. *[Nor are my efforts to control my twitching.]*

September 6, 9:51 a.m.

Gilbert: Hey, just seeing this message. I have been downstairs all morning, and I haven't heard him bark at all. *[I can recommend a good ENT doctor for you.]* Collar is charging now for good measure. *[Do you think that might be why Rocky is barking?]* Are you sure it is our dog that is barking? *[Are you kidding me?]* Sorry for the trouble.

September 6, 11:04 a.m.

Me: Everything is fine now. Thanks. The barking took place continuously between 6:00 a.m. and 7:30 a.m. I am quite sure it was your dog.

September 17, 7:38 a.m.

Me: Bad morning. I don't send you a message like this until the continuous barking exceeds thirty minutes. *[Twitch, twitch]*

September 17, 8:05 a.m.

Gilbert: I am not in town. The power company is working on the pole in front of the house directly in Rocky's line of sight. He is barking at the guys hanging out and "working." *[Gil, if you are out of town and you know all of this, then obviously someone is home. Are they semiconscious? Can't they hear the incessant barking?]*

September 17, 9:22 a.m.

Me: I guess the collar doesn't work in these situations. *[Especially if the people who are home don't bother charging it and putting it on Rocky.]*

September 17, 9:34 a.m.

Gilbert: The collar is a deterrent. It is not designed to prevent all barking. *[No, that would require a minimum amount of consideration on the part of your wife and children.]* Rocky is protecting his space and family. His barking deters people from coming onto the property. *[While driving the neighborhood mad.]* The house directly across the street from us is not inhabited and cars/trucks frequently congregate there. I will ask security to watch the space and keep it cleared. *[Please don't do that; then Rocky will bark at the security people.]* Rocky can see and hear these people as well as the people who exercise and walk their dogs in the morning.

September 18, 7:45 a.m.

Me: I understand that and appreciate your concern and help. However, there are lots of dogs in the neighborhood, and there are lots of people working and exercising. With respect, your dog seems to be the only one that responds to this by barking continuously for sometimes as long as an hour and a half. Invariably this occurs between 6 and 8 a.m.

October 3, 7:24 a.m.

Gilbert: FYI, I just thought I would let you know that we are working on finding a new home for Rocky. *[I immediately placed "Looking for Labrador" ads online and in all the local newspapers.]*

October 8, 8:20 a.m.

Gilbert: FYI, we have found Rocky a new home. From Sunday onward, the neighborhood should be quiet. I am in Tennessee right now. *[I hope Gilbert and Anita don't recognize me when they deliver Rocky to his new home.]*

It may have taken two years, but the neighborhood is now a hospitable place for misophoniacs.

• • •

T A K E
A H I K E

Six of us who had worked together ten years before in London, reunited at the home of our hostess, Diane, for a week's vacation on the beautiful island of Puerto Rico. A hike in El Yunque Rainforest was the activity for this day. After Diane served an ample tropical breakfast, the group bundled into a mini-van for a two-hour car ride to the rainforest. Upon reaching our destination, stomachs still slightly swollen from breakfast and restless from the long car ride, we bounded out of the vehicle with energy and enthusiasm to spare. Assembled at the base of the El Yunque trail, we prepared, with more activity than purpose, for a climb to the peak. But disappointment surfaced after opening the back of the car and discovering nearly everyone had left something at home: Ellen, her walking sticks, Diane, her rain jacket, and Peter, his sense of balance.

How could this be?

There was no mistaking the growing redness, part anger and part embarrassment, on the neck of Ellen, a veteran of hundreds of hikes who sheepishly admitted that she wasn't fully prepared. She paced, muttered, flailed, and the redness entered her facial area. She struggled for any explanation and then blamed her oversight, along with yesterday's inclement weather, on the recent election of President Trump.

Ellen, who always moves with speed and purpose, even when going nowhere, left no room for ambiguity about her political views, and regularly went to bed each night wearing the pink pussy hat she received at the Women's March on Washington.

Diane, a native Puerto Rican, had climbed El Yunque a dozen times before and was unlikely to have missed the none-too-subtle significance of the word rain in rainforest. More likely, she was overly preoccupied trying to figure out how to compress twenty-five hours of activity into a twenty-four-hour day for her guests for the remainder of the vacation. And if she managed to do that, she would get started working on squeezing in twenty-six.

Peter would explain his carelessness later. In contrast to Ellen—his wife of more than forty years—Peter is preternaturally calm, compelling his friends to check him periodically for a pulse, and while in the vicinity, a spine. The marriage has been a happy one, a salient feature being Peter's use of the phrase "Yes, dear," which he wields with uncommon dexterity and frequency. Just don't underestimate him. At first glance, one notices his embonpoint, and watching him trudge up a steep gravelly trail trying, always unsuccessfully, to catch up to his wife, makes one conclude that he would be more at ease in a Barcalounger than on a footpath. But he eventually finishes, as he almost always does, except for today.

By now the sky was changing fast, as it often does in a rainforest. The day's sunlight, which rarely reaches the forest floor, yielded to darkening clouds riding a wind that stayed above the tops of the densely packed trees, as close to each other as the planks of a picket fence. The moist air, which moments ago caressed our skin with warmth, now brought on goosebumps.

A light rain fell, much cooler than one would expect in the tropics, forcing us to don our rain jackets—except for Diane, of course, who having left hers at home, did jumping jacks to compensate.

After a quick stop at the restrooms, we began the hike, single-file along the narrow path. The trail was steep at the beginning, winding through vegetation so dense it acted like an opaque curtain denying us a scenic view of the lower elevation. Ten minutes had passed when we gathered to admire a small, but fast running, waterfall and stream. We needed this break to catch our breath and to drink some water. I handed out the water bottles from my backpack, and being nearest to Pippa, struck up a light conversation.

Pippa is an anomaly, being both warm and British, all at once. She is regal, but not haughty, and stands several inches taller than most people, which forces her to gracefully bend down to greet friends with a kiss, much the same way as the Queen gently tilts to greet her kneeling subjects.

No one has ever asked her to repeat herself. Her perfect enunciation makes that unnecessary. Somehow, our conversation turned to the political status of Puerto Rico. When I pointed out that the island was a Commonwealth of the United States, Pippa became animated, wanting to know more. As I explained further, she grew wistful, no doubt recalling past glories of the British Empire. But within minutes, she was hopping mad recalling how George III and his generals had squandered an overwhelming military advantage and lost the American colonies a few short centuries ago.

Rounding out the group was Robin, laid back and California cool, who is a huge asset for a taciturn person to have when forced to attend a dinner party. But on this day, Robin's loquaciousness and kick-back, West Coast manner had vanished, and she was spectral. It may have had something to do with receiving last rites from King Neptune, while clinging with one hand, one thousand yards from shore, to the last remaining rock in the area— all the other rocks, in fact, the entire coral system having being swept away by the current—and trying, with the other hand, to grasp Diane who had persuaded Robin to go snorkeling in the first place.

We resumed the hike, the path widening to allow walking two abreast. Diane and Ellen, deep in chatter about steps taken, calories burned, and pulse rates, set the pace for the group, unmindful of the rest of us and oblivious to the unique sights and sounds of this enchanting rainforest. Peter brought up the rear struggling to remain within binocular distance.

The soothing sound of a babbling brook and waterfall up ahead beckoned; the bridge over it would be our second rest and water stop. I handed out water bottles to everyone and took a long gulp from mine. Before I could finish, I heard a shriek from Pippa, and then a series of thuds and a splash. Pippa had dropped her plastic water bottle, which settled snugly between two rocks, twenty yards downstream from the bridge we were standing on.

In seconds, Peter snatched a rope from his backpack, tied one end to the bridge railing, the other around his waist, and rappelled down the stream, bounding off each moss-laden rock with such a light touch that he never slipped or lost his balance. He scooped up the water bottle, and with equal nimbleness, skipped his way upstream, hurdled the bridge railing, and landed to a hero's welcome, wayward bottle in hand. That, of course, didn't happen; just a bit of daydreaming on my part brought on by the high humidity and a spell of dizziness.

No, there the plastic bottle sat, unmoving, out of reach,

the only bit of refuse in the entire rainforest, glistening in the sunlight to remind us of our dereliction. And it would be there later that afternoon for viewing upon our descent, and perhaps another 4,352 years after that until it biodegrades.

We had a lot more climbing to do. Ellen and Diane again led, jabbering away as before, this time with Ellen practicing her language skills, grappling with the difference between the Spanish words for cramp and pumpkin (calambre vs. calabaza). Ellen was proud of the progress she was making and the level she had reached–after all, Diane had complimented her on it. I wasn't about to tell Ellen that Diane praises nearly every visitor she receives from the United States to make them feel at home in Puerto Rico.

We were nearing the summit, where a spectacular panorama awaited us if we could get there before some threatening clouds rolled in. Unable to keep up with Ellen and Diane's relentless pace, Peter now trailed the rest of the group by a full zip code. Just a few hundred yards from the peak, we found some flat rocks, sat down on them, and waited for Peter.

While waiting, we pondered that time- worn riddle: If a tree falls in the forest and no one is there, does it make a sound? Unbeknownst to us, Peter was testing this mystery at that very moment, tripping over an unseen rock, using his face to break the fall, and with a mouthful of dirt and leaves, calling out feebly, "Help." Because none of us heard it, we concluded that no sound had been made.

Peter limped his way up toward the summit. Fortunately, though bloodied and bruised, his condition was not serious, and at the summit, we discovered a small shed with an employee from the local electric company inside, and a car outside. I offered to pay the fellow to drive Peter down. When Ellen heard that I had paid him $40 for the service, she blurted out "I would never have paid him $40 for that!" which did little to speed up Peter's recovery from his physical injuries.

Eventually, but reluctantly, Ellen reimbursed me for the $40.

• • •

SPEECHLESS
AND UNBOWED

How could I say no to such a simple request by my niece for her wedding day?

The prospect of doing anything before an audience or in front of a group of people any greater than two unnerves me. Extemporaneous speeches are out of the question. The last time I was asked to do one, my pulse and blood pressure spiked in response to the terror engendered by the request. All my saliva vanished, leaving my tongue fastened to the roof of my mouth. With great effort and an audible clicking sound, I dislodged it, but only temporarily, as my tongue quickly returned to this unnatural resting place. If I had any chance at uttering a word, I would first have to coerce my tongue back to where it belonged. I tried again and again. Same result, same audible click. Instead of giving a heartfelt speech, I was standing before the crowd clucking like a chicken. I couldn't excuse myself because I couldn't say anything. So, I turned and walked out of the room, speechless, but still clucking.

More recently, a financial trade association pleaded with me to give a prepared speech. I insisted on at least one-month notice so I would have plenty of time to keep my mouth moistened. They agreed. Thirty days of near-sleepless nights preceded the big day. Already nervous, I consumed four cups of double espresso to remain awake and turned a mild tremble into spasmodic convulsions. My trousers had trouble remaining on my hips, falling nearly to my ankles before I noticed.

I had read that deep breathing helped calm the nerves before public speaking. I figured that if some deep breathing is good, more would be better. While waiting for the audience to settle and find their seats, I stood at the podium breathing deeply, slowly at first, then more briskly. But I seemed to be getting more nervous rather than less.

So, I sped up my rate of breathing until I noticed that a hummingbird flapping its wings outside a nearby window was having trouble keeping pace. I was taking enormous amounts of oxygen out of the room. The breathing did nothing to help my anxiety, but I did notice several people in the front row pass out from carbon dioxide poisoning. And the plants in the back of the room, which were waist-high when I arrived, were now scratching the ceiling, unable to control their photosynthesis process in the CO_2-rich auditorium.

Still shaking, I now had one hand on my trousers so they wouldn't fall. The other hand was on the podium so I wouldn't fall. I looked over the handwritten speech lying on the podium shelf and found parts of the document were illegible from smudge marks caused by a persistent drip of abnormally large drops of liquid. Strange, this was a brand-new auditorium. I glanced upward searching for a possible leak in the ceiling but found none. But I did find the source of the leak, my forehead.

I didn't want people to see me sweating or to know I was nervous. I wanted to wipe my brow as inconspicuously as possible. For this, I needed a free hand. So, I lifted my left leg until my knee was about belt high, and placed it firmly against the podium. This kept my pants up, freed my left hand, and gave me a chance to wipe my brow quickly and furtively. It seemed to work. No one noticed, although they couldn't help seeing the twin, eight-inch-wide arcs of sweat under each arm of the light-blue suit jacket I was wearing.

The crowd eventually settled. It was time to begin my speech. I finished my last bit of deep breathing, noticed some folks in the second and third rows lose consciousness, and wished I had brought a beach towel to the podium to wipe my brow. I noted the opening words of my speech—Good Morning—but was unable to say them because my tongue was stuck to the roof of my mouth.

Which brings me to my dear niece. Her marriage was to take place as part of a traditional Catholic Mass. All I have to do is to carry, at the appointed time, a saucer full of Communion hosts from the back of the Church to the priest who will be waiting at the altar in the front. I don't have to say anything. My tongue can happily remain affixed to the roof of my mouth without consequence. Yet, I was terrified. My niece assured me that it was nothing. Just remember to bow after I hand the saucer to the priest.

But what kind of bow? Should it be the *Eshaku*, the polite bow, or the *Dogeza*, the begging for your life bow, or one of the four bows between? What If I do the *Eshaku*, and the priest does the *Dogeza*? With 250 people in the pews watching? The embarrassment might demand that one of us perform *Seppuku*. And I hadn't yet paid the latest installment on my life insurance policy.

The wedding was forty days away, so I had plenty of time to practice the six standard bows. I did several thousand each night at home, and during the day, found myself bowing to the butcher and the barista behind the Starbuck's counter. With just two weeks to go, I did an all-nighter (of practice) at home. I pulled something in my back and after that, walked everywhere at a 45-degree angle.

I rented a tuxedo for the occasion and tried everything on but the shoes. Big mistake. Oh, they fit just fine, but I couldn't take a step without stopping short each time, nearly greeting the floor with my teeth. The soles stuck to everything. They seemed to be made of an advanced composite material from NASA's laboratories designed to prevent future astronauts from slipping on the Martian ice.

Wedding day arrived. I sat in a church pew, my eyebrows twitching and my knees bouncing. No one noticed the eye twitch but everyone in my row, growing queasy from the vibrating bench, sat forward and glared across at me, demanding with their eyes that I put my knees to rest. I didn't notice. But because I had my kneeler down and my quivering feet on it, everyone in the row in front of me was becoming dyspeptic. They looked backward, scowling. These people I noticed.

A few minutes before I was to carry the hosts, I rose and walked to the back of the church, much to relief of those sitting near me. There, I met the irritable middle-aged woman who was to give me instructions. She thrust the saucer into my hands, presumably miffed that I had not attended rehearsal. She said nothing. *So reassuring*, I thought.

I peered down the long, carpeted aisle to the altar. I couldn't erase an image of me sprawled out a couple of feet from where I was now standing, face down, eyeglasses mangled, hosts scattered on the nice rug, having been undone by the preternaturally sticky soles of my shoes. My reverie, or nightmare in this case, was pierced by the sudden bark of my drill instructor, who had tiptoed behind me until her mouth and my ear were only inches apart.

I think she said, "Don't screw it up." People who work in churches don't say things like that, do they? Unsettled to begin with, I jumped, yelped, and suffered an involuntary episode of flatulence, all at the same time. That was the first (and only) time I saw the church lady smile. My sudden movement caused several of the hosts to fly into the air, but I managed to catch all of them in the saucer with the skill of a pizza maker catching the tossed dough of a new pie being made.

Regaining my composure, I prepared myself for the long walk ahead, already feeling discomforted by the scrutiny of 500 eyeballs on me. It wasn't until now that I took a good measure of the priest. His head was bobbing. Was he doddering, or was he practicing the upcoming bow? I didn't recognize his bow; it was not in my repertoire. Could I learn it during the walk to the altar? To give me more time, I could ratchet down the pace of my walk to a shuffle, despite what the battle-ax in the back of the church had instructed.

Forty-eight minutes after taking my first step down the aisle, I arrived at the altar. I had learned nothing on the way down. The priest was as inscrutable as ever. Before I had a chance to hand the saucer to the him, he bows. Not a dodder, but a bow. Wait a second, the shrew told me the bowing comes *after* delivering the hosts. What should I do? Because the bow came unexpectedly, I didn't notice the type of bow it was. So I performed an *Eshaku*, a polite bow.

And the priest bowed once more. Why would he bow again? He must be telling me that I didn't demonstrate a proper level of deference, so I performed a lower, more respectful bow, a *Senrei*. But the priest bowed again. So, I bowed lower. This kept going a few dozen more times until I had gone through my entire arsenal of bows. I was now doing uber-*Dogezas*. I couldn't bow any lower without ripping up the floorboards and lowering my head into the crypt beneath the church.

This would have gone on forever, and my niece would have never gotten married, were it not for the alert altar boy who seized the saucer of hosts from me and handed it to the priest. With that, I was free to return my seat, which I did at a forty-five-degree angle.

• • •

SECTION 3

WHEN THE GOING GETS WEIRD, THE WEIRD TURN PRO

(WITH THANKS TO HUNTER THOMPSON)

The world has gone nutty. Needing perspective and logic to make sense out of current events, I dove into the Confessions of St Augustine. Failing to find answers there, I pored over the works of Kant and John Stuart Mill. Those, too, left me wanting. But I persevered, expanded my search, and the fog finally lifted. The world became a less inscrutable place when I discovered the philosophy of Inspector Clouseau.

THE
WAITING ROOM

My wife, Diane, didn't have much time to spare that day. She agreed to accompany me on an errand if we could get it done reasonably quickly. Every day is a full day for Diane, who abhors inefficiency and poor service, hates to waste time, and has the energy to make sure she doesn't. My mission this day was to secure approval to connect my company's newly installed solar panel energy system to Puerto Rico's electricity grid. This required the signature of the manager of the Utuado (a small town in Puerto Rico) office of the Puerto Rico Electric Power Authority (PREPA). Unsure of its precise location but quite sure that I lacked the Spanish language skills to accomplish my task, I beseeched my wife, who has a keen sense of direction and is a native Spanish speaker, for help.

Rarely, in today's hyper-connected world of the internet, cloud computing, and mobile phone apps for just about everything, does one find a relic of years past, but we found one in Utuado. It was as if, a generation ago, this office fell into some Jurassic Park–type amber, emerging only recently, protected from any technological contamination since its entombment.

The first thing I noticed when entering this office, apart

from the linoleum, the best-selling floor covering in the fifties, blighted with scuff marks from the shoes of that era, was the color gray— not a sleek, silver-gray, but a desolate, Mount St. Helens–after-the-eruption, volcanic-ash gray. Everything was gray: walls, ceiling, window frames, adding machines, steel desks and chairs— even the ashtrays, no longer used, but not yet discarded. The door had barely closed behind us when I noticed that Diane, after quickly sizing up the place, was becoming impatient, and she had developed a twitch that I had never before noticed.

The office was divided by a corridor bordered by floor-to-ceiling glass partitions that connected the front door to a fortified steel door about one hundred feet away. On the door, a large sign announced, in bold letters, "Authorized Personnel Only." It was printed in both English and Spanish to avoid any confusion. Los Alamos National Laboratory may have had fewer warnings. Something very important and secretive must have been taking place behind that door by some very important people. To the right of the corridor, straining to see through the glass made nearly opaque by age and lack of maintenance, I saw a large open area with five customer service windows in the rear, where two employees attended to a sinuous line of dozens of people waiting to pay their electricity bills. Most looked like farmers, the giveaway being the live roosters and hens in line with them, presumably to be used as barter for electricity. Direct debit was as alien to these folks as air travel was to cavemen. To the left of the corridor, another large room held about fifty metal chairs to accommodate the seventy-five to eighty people who were there with issues concerning their electricity account.

These customers were being underserved by the six customer service windows at the back of the room because there were employees behind only two of them. A flu bug going around Utuado? A handwritten sign taped to the glass divider identified this room as the "Waiting Room," a name which implied far more activity than seemed to be taking place and insulted the dynamism of waiting rooms everywhere. So torpid was this environment that local people have reported sightings of bears bringing their cubs there to prepare them for hibernation. After explaining our needs at the information desk, my wife and I were directed to the Waiting Room and instructed to take a number.

Diane's twitches became more pronounced.

Surveying the room, I noticed how docile, almost beaten down, everyone seemed, content to surrender huge chunks of their productive time to PREPA's ineptitude. I made some small talk with the fellow next to me, a middle-aged man, cleanshaven when he arrived, now with a Methuselean beard and working on his 584th Sudoku puzzle. He was unable to tell me how long he had been waiting. I inquired about the two people in the corner who appeared to be sleeping and was told they had died quietly earlier in the week. Wisely, I decided not to share this information with Diane, who was chatting irritably to a woman knitting a scarf now long enough to cover the necks of everyone in the room. We never looked directly at the people we were talking to, our gazes fixated on the two customer service windows for any perceptible evidence of progress. There was none. Then, I noticed chairs on both sides of the window, a nice customer service touch, although La-Z-Boys or convertible ottomans with bedding would have been more appropriate.

After listening with disinterest to the customer at the window, the employee on the other side would disappear for thirty minutes at a time, presumably to consult with the scientists who must have been behind the Authorized Personnel Only door. This happened just twice before Diane sprinted to the vacated window, yelling for the customer rep to return and demanding attention to our specific situation—the signature of the Head Scientist office manager.

Cutting into the line like this probably had never happened in the Waiting Room, even in the pre-amber days. I worried that our eighty roommates might rise from their lobotomized stupor in some real-life version of the Living Dead, and, I don't know, maybe eat us for jumping the queue. Miraculously, not only were we not consumed, but we were told to wait by the Authorized Personnel Only door, where a man appeared to tell us that the Grand Poobah office manager was at lunch (it was 11:00 a.m.) and that we should return at 2:30 p.m. Diane's twitches increased markedly, accompanied by wisps of smoke out of both ears. I suggested that we have lunch ourselves, wisely bundling her out of the building before she attempted to unscrew the hinges off the Authorized Personnel Only door and before the zombies started to chase us.

Diane's day was now shot, and I was the proximate cause. Our upcoming three- and-a-half-hour lunch together promised to be indigestible, at least for me. Attempting to soften the situation, I struggled to find an upscale restaurant in Utuado, but I found nothing more haute than a cafeteria that might do its best imitation of a Michelin star if only the owners knew what one was. I needed every minute of the three-plus hours to get Diane back on an even keel.

We returned to the elephant graveyard, opened the front door, and then dropped to our stomachs to slither through the corridor to avoid detection by the denizens of the Waiting Room. Arriving at the door marked Authorized Personnel Only, we stood and wiped off the grime on the front of our shirts and pants, to no avail, and knocked expectantly. The Grand Marshall office manager had not yet returned from lunch, came the reply. This posed a problem because we did not dare return to the Waiting Room, so we waited in line with the chickens in the bill-paying area.

About thirty minutes later, a functionary summoned us into the inner sanctum, where we discovered that Utuado was unaffected by the flu, with most of the town's population congregated—on the payroll, but not at work—behind the imposing door. What we saw inside was less imposing—dozens of steel desks and chairs, gray of course, people milling and talking to each other, the rotary telephones dead, the adding machines silent. The secret being kept here, better than Los Alamos kept its secret, was not that something important was taking place, but that nothing important was taking place. Finally, we were ushered into see the Lord High Priest of Everything office manager, a short, portly man by the name of Jose, who was having trouble breathing and speaking after four hours of dining.

Diane was anxious, irritated, and ready to pounce, but I counseled deference to this man who was managing such a large office, single-handedly responsible for its tempo. I kept the chloroform I brought ready for use should that become necessary.

Torpor of the kind afflicting Jose has its advantages. Uninterested, but mostly unable, to read the fine print, he quickly signed everything I put before him. By now, a commotion was developing outside the office. The zombies from the Waiting Room, resenting our preferential treatment, found out where we were and threw their bodies against the Authorized Personnel Only door.

Diane and I snuck out the back, leaving Jose, a potentially tasty treat, to confront the devouring herd.

• • •

SCHOOL
DAZE

Elementary school is a dangerous place. Only now do I realize the toll these early school years have taken on my physical, emotional, and psychological well-being. It didn't have to be that way, had my school put in place the proper safeguards many learning institutions do today. Because of my school's negligence, I now suffer from migraine headaches, I have difficulty sleeping through the night, and I tremble violently whenever I relive the frightful experiences of the past.

This unfortunate breakdown in my health has left me with no choice but to sue my elementary school, The Academy of Most Solemn and Holy Angels and Archangels in Heaven and a Few on Earth, for the irreparable emotional and psychological damages I am now suffering. I have assembled an expert, experienced legal team for this effort, and they must be top flight to deal with one especially inconvenient obstacle: my elementary school no longer exists, having closed its doors thirty years ago.

My psychiatrist says that it is therapeutic for me to confront the newly discovered horrors that preyed on me as a youth. Every day, it seems, I recall new examples of my school's negligence, increasing both my mental anguish and the frequency of my visits to the psychiatrist. Writing about them, as I do in this essay, not only helps me but, hopefully, countless others who suffer in silence, unable to make sense of the trauma that they are dealing with, and who perhaps might be willing to join me in a class action.

My legal complaint follows:

School in British Columbia bans holding hands; principal says it could put child at risk of injury.

In second and third grades, I was bewildered when my classmate, Bubba, who was much bigger than I, insisted on holding my hand. Then, it seemed inappropriate and unnatural, particularly when the other boys (and even some of the girls) taunted me. Now, I realize, thanks to the British Columbia school principal, the discomfort I felt was due to my fear of injury.

School in Washington bans swings; principal says they are the most unsafe of all playground equipment.

I can vouch for this. At my school, I spent a lot of time hanging around the swings, the centerpiece of our playground area. And so did young Maria Angelucci, who had a crush on me. One morning, our conversation was interrupted by Bubba demanding to hold my hand, prompting Maria to angrily push the swing at him. Bubba sidestepped the hurtling object, but I didn't. I received it with my head. No blood, but some dizziness that afternoon caused me to do poorly on a quiz, which depressed my grade point average, eliminated my chances of attending a top-tier university, and capped the potential of my future earnings stream.

School bans Wonder Woman lunchbox; principal deplores Wonder Woman as a person who solves problems using violence.

As I recall, Maria brought a similar lunch box to school, which undoubtedly accounts for her violent reaction to Bubba's interference. Had she been banned from bringing that lunchbox to school, she would not have tossed the swing at Bubba, saving my head from injury and allowing me to take that afternoon's quiz without dizziness, score a good grade, and ultimately prevent any loss of future earnings.

School in London bans "best friends"; headmaster says it could leave others feeling ostracized and hurt.

I sure could have used this fellow's enlightened thinking when Bubba declared me his best friend. I am unsure whether my classmates felt ostracized and hurt as much as they felt fear, but Bubba's actions were clearly putting a crimp on my social development.

School in Nebraska bans use of terms "boys" and "girls"; principal says important to celebrate gender diversity of all students.

With Maria wishing to hug me (now banned in many schools) at every opportunity, and Bubba lurking around every corner waiting to force me into holding his hand, I was having some difficulty understanding the meaning of the terms "boys" and "girls," not to mention the whole concept of gender.

School in New York bans backpacks; principal says can be used to conceal drugs, alcohol, and firearms.

Unfortunately, this is the only safeguard that elementary school had adopted, and it prevented me from bringing in the pepper spray I intended to use on Bubba the next time he grabbed my hand.

School in California bans wearing of American flag t-shirts on Cinco de Mayo but allows Mexican students to wear Mexican flag t-shirts; principal says did not want to offend "Mexican" students on "their day."

Every day, when I was in school, we sang the American national anthem and recited the Pledge of Allegiance to the US flag, even on the Italian Feast of San Gennaro. Rocco, Giuseppe, and I were never allowed to have "our day" to celebrate Italian customs, traditions, and great leaders like Dean Martin and Rocky Balboa. The three of us thought about hosting a culinary event for the class— spaghetti and meatballs—but we could never agree on whether the pasta should be cooked al dente or *alla gomma.*

School in Oregon bans peanut butter and jelly sandwiches; principal says they are a subtle form of racism and ties the sandwich to white privilege. Must be sensitive to "Somali or Hispanic students who might not eat sandwiches. Maybe they eat torta or pita."

What about the sensitivities of the Italians? All of this talk of PB&Js made Rocco, Giuseppe, and me feel ashamed of being seen in the lunchroom, huddled in a corner, eating a meatball hero (not sandwich), a block of provolone, and a few garlic breadsticks, which we washed down with three to four ounces of chilled Chianti. Anyone, white or otherwise, who regards a PB&J sandwich as a privilege over a meatball hero hasn't tasted my mother's cooking.

Not far from us were the Mexican students, sporting their Cinco de Mayo t-shirts, similarly ostracized as we were, lunching on pulled pork tamales with corn salsa and a side of guacamole picante.

School in Virginia bans packed lunches; principal says school lunches are healthier than lunch brought from home.

When I was in third grade, the meatball heroes stopped. There was a huge crackdown on the

Mafia that year, and in an odd coincidence, my uncle Sal, who was supporting our family financially, seemed to have lost his job. From that point on, my mother weakened me with a steady diet of liverwurst, olive loaf, spam, and baloney stacked limply on two pieces of the whitest of breads. Even today, we are not quite sure of the long-term effects of prolonged consumption of liverwurst and other processed "meats." But I am certain that had my school prohibited packed lunches, then I wouldn't be suffering from chronic intestinal flatulence since my teenage years.

School in Massachusetts bans Valentine's Day; principal says school has students of many nationalities and cultures; therefore, we shouldn't honor specific holidays.
Valentine's Day deprived me of that time of innocence when little boys admired the curls of little girls. In my elementary school, everyone brought Valentine cards and candy to school. No matter how many strings I tied on my fingers, I could never remember this date. So, when Maria, with a full heart, gave me her creative and painstakingly prepared card, and I delivered nothing, I encountered, well before my time, the scorn of a jilted female. This scenario played out annually from first grade to eighth grade, doing untold damage to my ability to secure and

maintain female relationships in later life.

School in Alabama bans Easter Bunny; principal says in the interest of religious diversity of students, no activities centered around any religious holiday will be allowed.

Bad enough, I was the last one of my classmates to realize that Santa Claus and the tooth fairy did not exist. Worse, was my unshakable belief in the existence of the Easter Bunny. If my school had the good sense to ban the Easter Bunny, it would have saved me from the hurtful snickering of my classmates and the cutting invective from Maria, who was still tormenting me for having missed Valentine's Day.

School in Washington bans tag; principal says ban will ensure the emotional and physical safety of all students.

Just good common sense from this observant principal. In my school, we played tag three times a day: in the morning before classes began, during lunch hour, and again at recess in mid-afternoon. I always participated with mixed feelings, knowing I was in emotional danger when Bubba was chasing me and physical danger when Maria was chasing me. Or was it the other way around?

School in Calgary bans academic honors and sports awards; principal says it hurts the self-esteem and pride of those who do not receive them.

Every year, my pride took a beating as I tried out for, but failed to make the school's baseball team. To make matters worse, the team regularly won the interscholastic league championship, receiving trophies, accolades, and the adulation of schoolgirls. The players were developing a measure of self-respect and confidence that they could rely on for the rest of their lives. Even Maria Angelucci deserted me in the fourth grade because of my continued inability to hit a curveball. I nearly won her back in sixth grade when I was a spare shy in the tenth frame of bowling 150 and winning a trophy, but I left a 7-10 split and ended with a score of 149.

In matters of academia, the honor roll proved elusive. If I couldn't remember Valentine's Day, what chance did I have remembering the key battles of the Revolutionary War? Although tutoring opportunities were offered after school, I never took advantage of them. I was too eager to get home to my bottle cap collection. Nevertheless, I felt the sting at the awards ceremony, when the principal decided that, to save time, she would announce the names of those who did not make the honor roll.

As comprehensive as my legal complaint already is, it will likely expand as new common-sense prohibitions at schools around the country emerge. In the meantime, The Academy of Most Solemn and Holy Angels and Archangels in Heaven and a Few on Earth, you've been served!

• • •

GET
SHORTY

On July 11, 2015, Mexico's most notorious drug lord, Joaquín "El Chapo" (nickname means "Shorty") Guzmán escaped from one of the country's highest security prisons. Authorities were both shocked and perplexed but shouldn't have been because Mr. Guzmán has done this sort of thing before. To provide the perspective needed for the casual reader, we bring you the official and unofficial account.

Mexico mounted an all-out manhunt for its most powerful drug lord, who escaped from Altiplano Prison. The elaborate underground escape route, allegedly built ~~without the detection of authorities~~ *(under the supervision of authorities)*, allowed Guzmán to slip out of one of the country's most secure penitentiaries for the second time. *(One can only imagine what the less-secure penitentiaries are like.)* "This represents an affront to the Mexican state," President Enrique Peña Nieto said, while on a previously scheduled trip to France. *(His whereabouts are now unknown; he is unlikely to return given reports that El Chapo was looking to settle a score for his imprisonment.)*

If Guzmán is not caught immediately, the drug lord will likely be in full command and control in forty-eight hours. *(This is backward; he has always been in control and is only now taking a forty-eight-hour vacation).* The Federal Attorney General's Office said that thirty employees from various parts of Altiplano Prison have been taken in for questioning *(and distribution of hush money)*. The United States had filed an extradition request, but then Mexican Attorney General Jesús

Murillo Karam scoffed at the idea, saying, "the US would get Guzmán after the 300 years he served in Mexican prison" *(his estimate being off slightly, by about 299 years).*

When the escape was discovered, a manhunt began for Guzmán, whose cartel is believed to control most of the major crossing points (and all the holes in the border fences) for drugs at the US border with Mexico. Guatemala's Interior Ministry reported that police and soldiers were keeping a close eye on Mexico's southern border for Guzmán *(while Guatemala's handsomely paid-off Immigration Ministry eagerly awaited El Chapo's arrival by air).*

Guzmán was last seen by the prison security-camera system in the shower area (after he bent down to pick up a bar of soap). Upon checking his cell *(two hours later—coincidentally the precise amount of time needed for Guzmán to complete packing his suitcase and to travel, by rail, through the tunnel),* authorities found it empty. Guzmán had climbed down a hole thirty-feet deep that connected with a tunnel approximately five feet six inches high *(El Chapo is five foot four, so no stooping would be necessary through the journey)* that was fully ventilated and had lighting. *(Authorities were appreciative that LED bulbs were used to save on energy costs.)*

A woman who lives close to the barn-like structure where the tunnel emerged said strangers bought the surrounding land *(for cash).* She said her son was employed as a construction worker on the site, and that the builders paid well *(although they overlooked issuing the Mexican equivalent of a W-2 Form at the end of the year).*

A seventy-four-year-old rancher, whose home sits between

the prison and the barn, not wanting to be named for safety reasons, said: "I didn't see anything strange" *(other than the steady sinkage of his home as dirt was removed from the tunnel being built directly under his property)*. "One day my cows wandered over to the barn," the rancher said, again repeating that he saw nothing strange. *(Most of his cows returned; only the ones that looked likely to divulge what they saw were detained by El Chapo's men.)*

Escaping from prison is not new to Guzmán, who escaped from the high-security prison Puente Grande in 2001. There are several versions of how he got away. Many accounts say he escaped in a laundry cart. *(More likely, Guzmán, dressed as a prison guard, was the one pushing the laundry cart with the unfortunate guard, whose clothes he had taken, gagged, and stuffed inside.)* What is clear is that he had help from other prison guards, who were prosecuted and convicted *(and then released, when the laundry cart was returned)*.

Upon hearing that El Chapo escaped, Donald Trump *(then the Republican presidential candidate)* who had previously categorized Mexican immigrants as rapists and drug dealers, wasted no time reminding voters of his toughness: "Can you envision Jeb Bush or Hillary Clinton negotiating with El Chapo? I, however, would kick his ass." When El Chapo tweeted that he would make Trump eat his words, tough-as-nails Donald implored the FBI for protection. *(Carlos Mendoza, Mexican American and son of Mexican immigrants, who heads the FBI's personal protection unit, was assigned to consider Trump's protection request.)*

• • •

WHERE'S
THE BEEF?

China may have to introduce carbon dating to its beef-aging process after news broke that traders have recently been peddling meat that was "more than forty years old." I enjoy aged beef, but as a general rule, I try to avoid beef that began its aging before the birth of my thirty-five-year-old son. On occasion, I will extend that limit to forty years, but "more than forty years old"? I think the risks are too great.

The normal aging process, a costly one that takes about a month or two, produces a delicacy served only in high-end restaurants and butcher shops. Presumably, this breakthrough in the lengthening of the aging process to four decades will further limit consumption to those with a billion dollars or two to spare—if they can only eliminate the stench of the meat. Forty years is a fairly long time, and perhaps not everyone involved along the way was as diligent as they should have been. Some, for instance, may have passed away during that period. This could result in the beef thawing and then being refrozen several thousand times. The aged beef was reportedly smuggled from Vietnam into China, where criminal masterminds figured they could improve their profit margins if they avoided the extra costs of using refrigerated trucks during transport, seemingly unbothered that anyone who comes within fifty feet of the beef throws up and then faints.

An expert on meat science at Colorado State University said it is possible for meat to last forty years when frozen. However, once it begins to thaw, the consumer will immediately know something is wrong: "The dead giveaway would be the odor and the taste." For me, the tip-off more likely would be the distinctive greenish-yellow hue and the community of maggots who, for 115 of their generations, had established a thriving colony in the meat in question.

China, no stranger to animal-food controversy, was also in the news recently when 15,000 dead pigs were found drifting down the Huangpu River in Shanghai. Authorities were befuddled about the cause of the porcine flotsam, but I think it was that ingenious entrepreneur who drove the unrefrigerated truck containing the forty-year-old beef.

He spotted an even more lucrative opportunity to save not only refrigeration costs, but also but also trucking costs by transporting the pork to market by river current. The Huangpu also just happens to be the main source of drinking water for more than 20 percent of Shanghai's twenty-three million people. Those same authorities, clueless about how the pigs got there, were unequivocal in their views about water quality, saying, "It is unaffected by the mass animal die-off and safe to drink."

Already nervous about my upcoming business trip to China, I read about several cases of meat-processing companies adding borax to pork to make it resemble beef. Or was it added to beef to make it resemble pork? Borax acts as a preservative and adds "a firm, rubbery texture to meat," an additive more suitable for automobile tires than for a main course. The real problem is that borax can be lethal, which these companies apparently haven't realized can limit repeat business.

I should probably stick to eating something safe and traditional while I am there, but I am worried that Chinese peanut butter might really be chicken made to look like peanut butter through the use of an additive. At least, I will be sure to avoid watermelons or at least those that are larger than a truck. Some farmers have been using copious amounts of growth accelerators causing these behemoths to explode, Hulk-like, from their skins ("Exploding Watermelons Put Spotlight on Chinese Farming Practices"). I don't want to get injured by a flying shard of watermelon shell and find myself in a hospital in Shanghai, where they serve drinking water from the Huangpu.

• • •

THANK YOU, RACHEL

I always had a tough time in school. When I was young, my teachers forced us to sit in a corner of the room and wear a dunce cap when we didn't have the right answers to their questions. Unable to master the multiplication tables, I frequented that corner. Sporting that cap was only slightly less humiliating than wearing a scarlet letter. My grades were always poor. My IQ and SAT scores were below average. I had trouble with math, English, history, and everything else. Rejected by every college I applied to, I attended a nondescript community college, and, even there, finished in the bottom 25 percent of the class. After graduation, job-market opportunities for me were limited because the high-paying, rewarding ones always went to those with better grades.

For many years, I suffered in silence in a society that discriminated against, and was hostile to dim-witted people. Until Rachel Dolezal, head of the NAACP's Spokane, Washington, branch, courageously stepped forward and declared, "I identify as black." With Rachel blazing the path forward for me, I decided to step forward and banish years of discrimination and humiliation and declare: "I identify as intelligent." Rachel says she started identifying herself as black around age five when she drew self-portraits with a brown crayon. I had a remarkably similar experience. At around age six, I drew self-portraits as a tenured professor with an endowed chair at Harvard, although I don't recall the color of the crayon I used.

I always felt like an intelligent person trapped inside a feeble-minded brain and body, and I am hoping my actions, as perhaps the first trans-intellectual, will provide positive help to teenagers who are struggling with their intellectual identity. I used to cross-intellectualize in the privacy of my home, imitating the cerebral members of society, where I did word-search puzzles, three-letter word jumbles, kid's Sudoku, and surfed Mensa's website. But no longer. Now that I declared, I feel liberated. I regularly use unfamiliar words in social gatherings without feeling uncomfortable. I even thought about having an operation to have more brains added, but the doctors told me it was too risky because my head isn't large enough.

Am I a hero? Yes. Anyone who comes out like this is heroic when one considers that trans-intellectual people routinely face job discrimination, condescension, and bullying. I am a role model to young people. I am demonstrating how to do something society may tell them is impossible. I probably won't win an ESPY award for courage, but I am told that the Nobel Prize committee is favorably disposed toward my prospects of receiving its award.

• • •

HOLY GUACAMOLE, BATMAN!

(written during the 2016 Presidential primary)

Republican presidential candidate Donald Trump launched his campaign with his usual brashness, declaiming that illegal Mexican immigrants—most of whom are criminals, rapists and drug dealers—are ruining America. Wasting no time, Democratic presidential candidate Hillary Clinton, wearing a sombrero, held a townhall meeting where tacos, enchiladas, and extra spicy tapas were served. She followed this with a series of press conferences held at El Pollo Loco.

In response to Mr. Trump's insensitive comments, Univision dropped its sponsorship of the Miss Universe Pageant, partially owned by Trump. Mexico withdrew its candidate to the pageant, and Macy's dumped the Trump name on some of its ties and button-down shirts.

Who buys Donald Trump ties and shirts anyway? Shampoo or hair dryers, maybe, but menswear? Macy's reintroduced all clothing and accessories having the Trump name as the Pancho Villa Collection. Mrs. Clinton immediately instructed the Clinton Foundation to take a sizable equity stake in Macy's and offered Carlos Slim a position on the Clinton Foundation Board.

Meanwhile, Chipotle Mexican Grill and Taco Bell banned the Donald from their restaurants for life. The PGA Tour, which runs a World Golf Championship at the Trump Doral near Miami, declined to comment on whether Trump's remarks would affect their relationship with him. Their reticence was probably due to their earlier allowing sex-crazed Tiger Woods to remain on tour. In a rare display of unity, several warring Colombian drug lords issued a scathing press release criticizing Trump for discriminating against Colombia's US drug business by giving all of the credit to the Mexicans. It is rumored that Colombia, too, will be withdrawing its Miss Universe candidate, who is allegedly being held in an undisclosed jungle location by one of the cartels.

As expected, Trump filed a $500 million lawsuit against Univision, citing breach of the Miss Universe contract and an infringement of his First Amendment right to eat at Taco Bell. In a bid to bolster his flagging Latino support, Trump pledged that half of the proceeds from the lawsuit would be used to buy toilet paper for Venezuela. Trump claimed the true motive for the breach by Univision was its support for Hillary Clinton. Univision countered that the lawsuit was legally ridiculous and "factually incorrect" since they support Native American Senator Elizabeth Warren for president.

In related news, Trump had a campaign staffer carefully review recently released emails from Hillary Clinton's private server. The staffer uncovered one where Mrs. Clinton advised her campaign manager, John Podesta, to wear socks to bed. Not wishing to lose any edge to his opponent, Mr. Trump was spotted at ~~Macy's~~ JC Penney buying hosiery for his campaign manager and an extra hair dryer for himself. In a second email, Clinton asked aides for restaurant recommendations, Mexican only, for dinner with California Democratic Senator Dianne Feinstein. Trump responded by making reservations at his favorite steakhouse for dinner with some of the border guards who have been advising him on Mexican immigration movements.

The candidates can be mystifying. One day, Mr. Trump characterizes Mexican immigrants as drug dealers, criminals, and rapists, and then says, "I love the Mexican people. I've had a great relationship with Mexico and the Mexican people."

For her part, Mrs. Clinton can also be difficult to understand. "I think we have to speak out against it," Clinton explained. "Everybody should stand up and say that's not acceptable." At first, this was thought to be her reaction to State Department approval (while she was Secretary of State) of selling American uranium mines and exploration fields to the Russians soon after the sellers and the Russians made sizable "donations" to the Clinton Foundation. Only later it was discovered that those comments were in response to reports that someone had stolen Mr. Podesta's socks.

The cost of running a campaign, at record levels, four years ago was even higher for this election. With several dozen Republican presidential candidate opponents and the formidable Clinton in the finale, Trump needed to count on his net worth being the $9.4 billion he reminds everyone every hour or so, and not the $1.84 estimated by *Forbes* magazine. As for Clinton, she must hope that husband Bill continues to land $100,000 speaking engagements from Russians intent on buying American uranium assets.

• • •

GENDER
JOLLIES

Born too late. My friends and I were born a generation too late, and we can only dream of how Title IX legislation—and its broad interpretation—would have changed our lives in high school and college. For eight years, we guys conspired to get a peek into the girls' bathroom, staying after school, armed with cafeteria spoons and pocket knives, boring strategic holes in the bathroom wall. Had he been around at the time, President Obama would have laughed at our secret peepholes because he authorized today's high school and college boys to simply walk through the bathroom door with the skirt marked on it and take a look around. My friends and I would have pegged Mr. Obama as the greatest president since Abraham Lincoln and been eager to overturn the Twenty-Second Amendment to vote him in for a third term.

Here is how I imagine it would have been.

"Hey, have you seen this?" said my friend Sam, motioning for us to put down our cafeteria spoons and pocket knives for a moment. In his hand, was a five-page directive, dated May 13, 2016, signed by the US Department of Justice and Department of Education, which he begged us to read. Annoyed by this distraction from the important work at hand, we reluctantly did as he instructed. Sam would later recount how our facial expressions changed from disdain to wonderment. For nearly an hour, we studied, parsed, and memorized every word and phrase, faster and more precisely than we had any Shakespearean sonnet. The things you don't learn in school.

For example, gender identity. The directive tells us that "gender identity refers to an individual's internal sense of gender. A person's gender identity may be different from, or the same as, the person's *sex assigned at birth*." That last phrase in italics threw us off. Sex assigned at birth? It sounded very much like the way a summer camp counselor assigns pre-teen campers to the Chipmunk Cabin or the Gator Cabin.

But we were too excited about now having the ability to choose our gender to worry about sex assignments at birth. To help us with the gender-selection process, we watched the movie *What Women Want* (several times) and read and reread *6 Ways to Get in Touch with Your Feminine Side*. Then, we got busy contacting our family doctors to persuade them to give us a doctor's note asserting our new gender identities. But that was clearly unnecessary per the directive: "There is no medical diagnosis or treatment requirement that students must meet as a prerequisite to being treated consistent with their gender identity." Almost seems like we wrote the directive ourselves.

Initially, we were a little tentative, so we wore lipstick around school for a few weeks before using the ladies' room. But upon careful rereading of the directive—"transgender individuals may undergo gender transition at any stage of their lives, and gender transition can happen swiftly"—we realized that all we had to do was swiftly splash on a little perfume a few minutes before entering the girls' bathroom. Word got out to the football team, after which I noticed some of the offensive line wearing makeup and sneaking in as well. They were soon followed by a couple of running backs and the starting safety. Before long, most of the team was in there, and not only did they not bother with makeup, they went in wearing shoulder pads and cleats. One of the girls in the bathroom went to the practice field looking for the coach to complain, but she couldn't find him there because he, too, was in the ladies' room.

To no one's surprise, the boys' bathroom wasn't getting much use, so little that the administration was able to cancel the janitorial services. One of our teachers, a priest (my school was Catholic) who frequently hung around the boys' bathroom because of a professed urinary problem, wondered, ever since the directive was issued, where all the boys were.

After a few months, the girls' bathroom got a little boring, so back to the directive we went, and bingo! Our hands were shaking when we read that "transgender students must be allowed to access such facilities—locker rooms and showers— consistent with their gender identity." No longer did we have to enroll in ballet classes. Instead, we all switched majors to physical education and requested approval for course overload. In the interests of proper hygiene, we showered after every class.

Again, word got out, and soon the entire football team— including the taxi squad and the coach—were taking showers in the girls' locker room. They were closely followed by the priest, now cured of his urinary problem, but claiming the emergence of a skin condition that required frequent showering. Within weeks, English, history, and business majors dried up, while requests for enrollment in phys ed majors were done by lottery. Many female students protested to the administration, but school officials brushed them off, citing the directive: "A school may not discipline students or exclude them from activities for behaving in a manner that is consistent with their gender identity."

The protesting girls said they felt ill at ease taking a shower next to a football player, but the head of administration responded testily, again quoting the directive: "The desire to accommodate others' discomfort cannot justify a policy that singles out and disadvantages a particular class of students." One of the girls asked why the logic doesn't work both ways, i.e., the desire to accommodate other's (transgender females') discomfort (taking showers with males) cannot justify a policy that singles out and disadvantages a particular class of students (non-transgender girls). The head of admin listened, scratched her head, and said she was late for her next meeting.

Just when my friends and I thought things couldn't get any better, they did. We discovered that the directive—that Magna Carta of documents—compelled schools to allow transgender students access to, not only, bathrooms, locker rooms, and showers, but housing, as well. We applied fresh coats of lipstick, bought some pom-poms, and brought our request to transfer to the girls' cheerleading team's dormitory to Mrs. Anita Rodrigues, the person in charge of Student Services.

Mrs. Rodrigues didn't appear to be aware of the directive and gave us the impression of being socially conservative. While watching Mrs. Rodrigues slowly shred our request, we introduced her to the directive. We pointed to the section which read, "A school's failure to treat students consistent with their gender identity may create or contribute to a hostile environment" and mentioned that we weren't big on hostility.

With unconcealed contempt, she spat out: "Listen, Robert, Joseph, Sam, and George," but we again interrupted her, citing the directive: "School staff and contractors will use pronouns and names consistent with a transgender student's gender identity." We gently informed her that we preferred to be addressed as Roberta, Josephina, Samantha, and Georgette, so that we could, you know, avoid that dreaded hostility thing. Her anger building, Mrs. Rodrigues called her assistant and instructed her to examine our personnel files, but we demurred, pointing out that the directive says, "Non-consensual disclosure of personally identifiable information such as a student's birth name or sex assigned at birth, could be harmful to, or invade the privacy of, transgender students."

Within a week, Mrs. Rodrigues was reassigned to a different department and was seen attending sensitivity-training classes. And within a month, not only was I living in the cheerleaders' dormitory, but I was placed into a forced triple with Tracy and Barbie, the team's co-captains. Life was good, with only one complication. Around the time that grades were issued, I had to switch back to the sex I was assigned at birth because my class ranking would be lower if I were included in the female population where the grade point averages were higher.

Alas, none of the above happened while we were in school. Richard Nixon was president, Barack Obama wasn't yet a teenager, the prized directive wasn't due for another forty years. So, we continued to burrow away at the bathroom wall with our cafeteria spoons.

• • •

LATTE SALUTE: THE UNTOLD STORY

Once again, conservatives and Republicans criticized President Obama, this time over his apparent salute to Marines with a cup of latte in his hand while disembarking from the presidential helicopter Marine One. The event has been dubbed "the Latte Salute." Officials traveling with the president shot back at the critics for again savaging the president without having all of the facts and informed them that Mr. Obama was carrying a cappuccino, not a latte.

Sources said that the president was battling a mosquito throughout the flight, and the mosquito landed on the right side of his forehead just as he was disembarking. What looked like a salute was really a determined commander in chief showing that insubordinate mosquito who was in charge by squashing it on the presidential temple. For a nation that admires vigorous leaders and looks for energy in the executive, the president was irked that the press ignored the athleticism of the moment—descending stairs, carrying a hot cup of coffee—without a protective sleeve, mind you, while swatting a mosquito, all done without spilling a drop of cappuccino. Could President Ford have done that? Or President Reagan in his second term?

President Obama, a fastidious user of bone china, was also not happy at the potential damage to his pro-environmental image by being seen carrying a paper cup (loss of trees) with a plastic lid (non-biodegradable). An unnamed official blamed this unfortunate turn of events on a brigadier general on-board Marine One. After a lengthy briefing of the president on the situation in Ukraine, which prevented President Obama from getting any sleep, the general was directed by the president to make a latte to try to compensate for the foregone slumber. After several failed attempts, just as Marine One was landing, the hapless general managed to produce a cappuccino, instead of the requested latte. And because the president needed it "to go," the general's handiwork had to be placed in one of those paper cups detested by the commander in chief.

According to a spokesman, President Obama was determined to overcome these coffee frustrations and decided that as he was disembarking, he would take a moment to address the waiting media. He planned on exhorting the nation to follow Michelle's nutritional message from her Let's Move program. And he would take a leadership role by switching from whole milk to 2 percent in his lattes. But he never got a chance to deliver that message, undone by that pesky mosquito.

• • •

FAST BREAK IN
PYONGYANG

Napping is a high-risk activity in North Korea as the former, now vaporized, Defense Minister Hyon Yong-chol found out after falling asleep during a meeting held by Kim Jong-un, North Korea's Supreme Leader. Mr. Hyon, already cranky from having been awakened prematurely from his nap, was even more cranky when told he would be executed by an anti-aircraft gun, normally used to shoot objects five miles distant, from one hundred feet away. Imports of NoDoz tablets and Red Bull energy drinks into Pyongyang have since skyrocketed.

Mr. Kim's tetchiness probably stems from a difficult childhood, marked by the absence of a warm relationship with his father, Kim Jong-il, whom no one is quite sure ever uttered a word as an adult. Reputedly, the father never had to use the bathroom, which some people believe pointed to his divine powers; others claim he simply used the woods behind the presidential palace. In any event, it was enough to confuse his son during his potty-training days, undoubtedly leaving psychological scars of unknown severity.

Classmates and teachers at the prestigious Liebefeld-Steinhölzli boarding school near Bern described the young Jong-un as socially awkward and intellectually dull but obsessed with basketball, despite being unable to hit free throws and turning over the ball too much. His inadequacies on the court, difficult enough to bear, were magnified by the sports accomplishments of his father, a golf prodigy who according to reliable (ahem) North

Korea news reports shot 38 under par, including eleven holes in one, the first and only time he played a round of golf.

Upon assuming power after his father took ill and died, the diminutive new leader, listed at five foot two but really just a shade taller than four foot seven, was instantly acclaimed as the best basketball player in the ~~country world~~ universe. Sports news from the secretive country revealed that Mr. Kim was not only winning every dunk contest held in North Korea, but displayed his jumping ability by retrieving dimes, or their North Korean equivalent, placed on the top of the backboard. This latter feat was confirmed by dozens of eyewitnesses who are under continuous surveillance and are permanently strapped to remote-controlled explosives.

The United States, not believing these reports and eager to discredit the North Korean leader and nation, had a difficult time deciding whether to send Dennis Rodman or Donald Trump to observe Mr. Kim on the court. Dennis it was, but the hallucinogens that Rodman was using at the time may have affected his evaluation of Mr. Kim's leaping prowess. In a debriefing by the State Department upon his return to the United States, Rodman mumbled incoherently something about the rim being set at two foot seven. However, state officials were unable to concentrate, distracted by the wedding dress and veil Dennis wore to the debrief. The next stop on Rodman's sports diplomacy tour will be Venezuela, bringing with him several rolls of Scott's toilet paper as a gift to President Nicolás Maduro. Rodman will do an in-depth study of the country's Ministry of Supreme Social Happiness.

Defense Minister Hyon hasn't been the only person in the

Hermit Kingdom to run afoul of its newest Dear Leader. Mr. Jang Sung-taek, Mr. Kim's uncle, was allegedly executed by a pack of 120 crazed dogs. Reports indicate that this was a typical move by Kim to consolidate power, but others believe the particularly nasty method of execution was payback by Kim for having been benched by Jang, then coach of Kim's basketball team, following a missed free throw in a league game. Tryouts start soon for the administration's Organization and Guidance Department of the Workers' Party basketball squad. Mr. Kim will play four out of the five positions at the same time. His teammates can use the barking sounds of 120 dogs outside the arena to help them concentrate on making their foul shots.

• • •

PROFILES
IN COURAGE

Emory University is considerably less safe after student Horace Shufflebottom wrote Donald Trump's name in chalk on various parts of the campus early this morning around 1:00 a.m. The pallid, five-foot five inch, 135-pound, Shufflebottom, unnoticed during daylight hours, now competes with Son of Sam and Jack the Ripper in inspiring fear. Dozens of students at Emory now walk to their classes furtively looking over their shoulders, an instinctive reaction to the uncontrollable fear that Shufflebottom and his malignant chalk may be lurking in the shadows.

Within hours of the pernicious chalk markings having been spotted, nearly one hundred students organized a protest and marched to the university president's office chanting, "Come speak to us. We are in pain." The president wasted no time in hiring an expert in pain management, who, after diagnosing the condition as phantom pain, began applying deep brain stimulation to the suffering students. Should that fail to alleviate the symptoms, opioids would be distributed, but only to those having GPAs of 3.4 or higher.

As the students milled about in front of the president's office, one young woman, who said "I don't deserve to feel afraid at my school," was commended by the president for her humility. Another student said, "I legitimately feared for my life," while unwittingly standing next to the spectral Shufflebottom himself, who had quietly joined the protest.

A third student was in pain and feared for his life because

Trump is "a figurehead of hate, racism, xenophobia, and sexism in America." The president thought about sharing his own, much more painful college experience of having to endure chalk markings all over campus saying "Archie Bunker 1976." However, he didn't want to exacerbate the already profound pain of the students. Besides, the supply of pain-killing opioids was limited.

Addressing the group, Dylan, the bespectacled student leader of the protest, and a paradigm of courage, said, "We are not afraid of chalk!" He began a discourse that mesmerized the student audience, who intently followed his every word as he recounted how he vanquished his fears of the boogie man in his bedroom closet several months before he entered college.

After Dylan spoke, the crowd again became restless and challenged the president, saying that inaction by the administration against the Trump chalkings was the equivalent of supporting Trump's messages. The president responded by calling out, Pontius Pilate–like, to the protesters, "What actions should I take?"

A few students said, "Provide free chips when ordering a supersized hero at the Student Center."

"What else?" yelled the president. "Should we ban Trump supporters from campus?"

In unison, the students whooped, "Yes!"

The president continued, "Shall I build a wall around campus to keep Trump supporters from entering?"

Another boisterous "Yes!" from the students.

With the protest still bubbling, the president drafted and released a statement: "During our conversation, the students voiced their genuine concern and pain in the face of the perceived intimidation" caused by having to see the chalked message "Trump 2016" on campus.

Bowing to further pressure from the students for action, and especially concerned about the intimidation factor, he contacted the local high-security prison and arranged for the temporary release of a 6-foot, 7-inch snarling gentleman named Psycho to give students counseling on the differences between real and perceived intimidation. At this point, a few students said, "It is our duty to fight for our freedom. It is our duty to win. We must love each other and support each other. We have nothing to lose but our chains."

The president responded by promising to have a table set up outside his office with ROTC application forms for those who felt a duty to fight for freedom. He also agreed to bring back Psycho to compare his experiences of being chained to those of the students. The group kumbaya session continued with the assistant vice president for community (no wonder tuition costs have skyrocketed) praising the protest for giving her "greater insight into the pain that some students experienced as a result of the chalkings."

This prompted another student, Jamie, to step forth and unburden himself, spouting some solipsistic drivel that should alarm the Registrar's Office about whether its stated intellectual requirements for admission to the school are being enforced. Jamie said, "When I saw a chalking saying 'Trump 2016,' I thought nothing of it. But when I saw a chalking saying 'Accept the Inevitable: Trump 2016,' that was a bit alarming. What exactly is inevitable? Why does it have to be accepted?" Again, the ever-

responsive president stepped in and promised extra tutoring
sessions in vocabulary, with special emphasis on teaching the
meaning of such words as inevitable. He also agreed to establish
free refresher courses in civics and government to remind students
that presidential candidates do not attain office through chalk
markings.

The university will review footage of security cameras
to identify those who made the chalkings, the president told the
protesters. If the culprits are students, they will go through the
conduct violation process and be subjected to intense sensitivity
training. A review of the tapes was done, and unfortunately for
Shufflebottom, he starred in the security film.

The president summoned Shufflebottom to his office
and accused him of violating the campus chalking policy, which
he enunciated for Shufflebottom's benefit. "Chalking must be
reserved and approved by Emory's campus reservation service.
Chalk cannot be on columns or walls; it must be done on
horizontal, ground surfaces and areas where rain can easily wash
it away. Chalking may only remain for forty-eight hours. After this
time, another group can chalk, if they reserve their chalking with
Emory's reservation service."

The president then delineated each of Shufflebottom's
violations of policy: failure to make a proper reservation; failure
to write on horizontal surfaces only; failure to ensure that it rained
within forty-eight hours to wash away his chalkings. In addition,
the president noted that Shufflebottom, by supporting a candidate
who is "a figurehead of hate, racism, xenophobia, and sexism"
inflicted profound pain on hundreds of students and intimidated

hundreds of others by displaying that support via his "Trump 2016" chalking. And to make matters worse, Shufflebottom used only white chalk instead of using chalks of color.

The president said he had no choice but to order two hundred hours of sensitivity training for Shufflebottom, beginning with watching fifty hours of *The Honeymooners* to observe that menacing sexist, Ralph Kramden, who regularly threatened his wife with a clenched fist and the threat, "Oh Alice, you're gonna get yours!" This session would be followed by watching the movie, *White Men Can't Jump*, for twenty-four hours straight, to be scheduled on election day to prevent Shufflebottom from voting for a candidate whose "platform and values undermine Emory's values."

Sensing that Shufflebottom's punishment might not be enough to appease the student protestors, the president considered a modified form of waterboarding if agreed to by a majority of protesters. The students' support was unanimous. Since meeting with the president, Shufflebottom's whereabouts are unknown. Rumor has it he has quit Emory and opted for homeschooling

• • •

THROUGH THE LOOKING GLASS

Say what you want about former bus driver, now president of Venezuela, Nicolás Maduro's economic program, but timidity will not be a term used in that conversation. His ingenuity and boldness in dealing with product shortages, raging inflation, and currency devaluation will require drastic revisions to economic theory and textbooks everywhere.

When word leaked that three-dozen 747 cargo planes, presumably loaded with scarce foodstuff and personal items, were on their way to product-deficient, inflation-ravaged Venezuela, thousands of people swarmed to the airport in anticipation. Authorities, fearful that unrest and violence might ensue when the cargo of newly printed 50 and 100 Bolivar notes were unloaded, were surprised by the appreciation expressed by the crowd that the toilet paper shortage was, at last, being addressed.

More recently, to save dwindling reserves of energy, President Maduro pronounced that, henceforth, Friday would be a holiday. "We'll have long weekends," Mr. Maduro excitedly declared, assuring everyone that the holiday applies only "to public workers who won't adversely affect production with their absence." This statement puzzled many because no one in Venezuela has produced much of anything for quite some time.

"Hotels and malls are being asked to use generators on Fridays," Mr. Maduro said, but will, of course, fully recharge them using electricity on Saturday. As a result of this policy change, the president pointed out that the expression "Thank God it's Friday" will be officially changed to "Thank God it's Thursday."

Many of President Maduro's other energy-saving and product-shortage relief measures do not garner the headlines that Friday Fiesta did. Last month, the president banned the watching of TV on even-numbered days but learned that rampant cheating was taking place. His chief aide, Mr. Ubaldo C., who suggested that the ban would be far more effective if the state nationalized all TV stations and broadcast only Maduro's speeches 24/7, has vanished. Eventually, the government did just that. Not only did the compliance rate rise to 100 percent on even-numbered days, but it hit 100 percent on odd-numbered days as well.

President Maduro encouraged people to grow food and raise chickens in their homes, even though 83 percent of Venezuelans live in cities. To help them, Mr. Maduro announced the formation of a Ministry of Urban Farming. The president claims that he and First Lady Cilia Flores have taken up the cause, and have sixty laying hens. "We produce everything we eat," Maduro said in a speech. Unnamed sources close to the president say that Mr. Maduro knows absolutely nothing about farming (among many other things), and they have pointed out that Mr. Maduro's statement is technically true, since the president and his wife haven't eaten anything but eggs for two months.

The Venezuelan president also urged women to stop using hair dryers in a desperate bid to tackle the energy crisis. "I always think a woman looks better when she just runs her fingers through her hair and lets it dry naturally. It's just an idea I have," he said. This idea he had didn't last very long. The president quietly and quickly dropped it after spending five restless nights sleeping on the couch in the servants' quarters, having been banished from the presidential bedroom by the first lady.

Most people would take great comfort in knowing that the president and his vaunted team of fecund economic experts were hard at work devising additional energy-saving and shortage-relief measures to be rolled out if existing ideas such as longer weekends don't produce satisfactory results. Among the most promising ideas are:

> - Abolish Thursdays. Not only would this save energy, but it would improve the shortage situation. Instead of most food and personal items being available in the supermarkets only once a week, now they would be available once every six days.

> - Institute Daylight Diminishing Time. Days would start at 11:00 a.m. and end at 3:00 p.m. Everyone must wear very dark sunglasses before 11:00 a.m. and after 3:00 p.m. in case the sun fails to cooperate with this new proclamation. Businesses may operate only during the new daytime, thereby leading to huge savings in electricity. All of the country's roosters will be required to be sent to the newly created Ministry of Daylight Diminishing Time for retraining to learn to crow each morning around 11:00 a.m.

- In a Facebook post recently, Mr. Maduro hinted at disputes among his Ministers, one of whom, Mr. Ugueth M., argues that inflation does not exist. In another display of his ability to block out all aspects of reality, Mr. Ugueth unveiled a novel idea, strongly supported by the president: Shut off traffic lights throughout the country every two hours for thirty minutes. At such times, all cars and trucks must shut off their engines and remain in place. This measure would not only save electricity, but also gas, and as a byproduct, would improve the quality of the air.

- Ban the use of electric can openers. This proposal would yield significant energy savings if there were any cans of anything left on the supermarket shelves. The idea was suggested by—you guessed it—Minister Ugueth, who, in addition to not believing that inflation exists, doesn't believe that there are any shortages either.

- If the toilet paper shortage re-emerges after all of the new Bolivar notes have been used, then the government will issue two squares of toilet paper to each citizen on odd-numbered days. To add teeth to the measure, the government will also ban the use of the toilet on even-numbered days.

- To complement the new Ministry of Urban Farming, the president would create the Ministry of Ideas of Former Bus Drivers. The president, closely involved in the work of this ministry, has mandated its staff to develop a micro-hydropower device to be distributed to each household and attached to every toilet bowl in the country. These devices, in turn, will be connected to the country's electricity grid. Once they are installed, the entire population will be required to flush their toilets twice a day (odd-numbered days only) at precisely 11:30 a.m. and 6:12 p.m. Mr. Ferdinand H., who holds the coveted directorship of this new agency, estimates that this project will replace 80 percent of the hydropower lost to El Niño weather conditions.

- The president and his advisers were baffled as to why the Vice Ministry of Supreme Social Happiness, created by Mr. Maduro in 2013, had not produced better results for the country. After extensive analysis and discussion, they concluded that its performance would be substantially improved by elevating it from a Vice Ministry to a Full Ministry, and by changing its name to the Ministry of Sublime Intergalactic Jubilation. One additional measure, still being considered is authorizing the ministry to dispense marijuana and mind-altering mushrooms to any citizen who presents a doctor's note documenting his or her unhappiness.

- The proximate cause of the energy crisis is the El Niño–induced drought that has crippled Venezuela's energy production, 60 percent of which comes from hydroelectric power. Thinking logically, President Maduro gathered his uber intellectual cabinet ministers for a meeting and challenged them to develop ideas on how to alter the El Niño current. An uneasy silence followed, but none of the ministers dared confront Mr. Maduro.

- They recalled that shortly after formally taking office, he claimed to have seen the late Hugo Chavez in the form of a bird flitting around the presidential palace. Many Venezuelans, although they haven't seen the Chavez bird personally, have seen many samples of the excrement which that bird has left behind. Most of the cabinet meeting was spent discussing the solution passionately put forward by the president: dispatch a flotilla of rowboats into El Niño waters with instructions to coordinate their paddling to rechannel the current into a direction more likely to stimulate precipitation. Unanimous agreement on the idea

was achieved, with the only outstanding issue still
to be settled being the number of rowboats to
include in the flotilla.

Most of the citizens of Venezuela are cheered that Horatio Alger-
type success opportunities exist in their country—that a bus driver
can aspire to and attain the presidency. They wish, with equal
fervency, that there are even greater opportunities for this journey
to be taken in the opposite direction.

• • •

" H I G H E R "
E D U C A T I O N

To me, a college education was no different from purchasing any other consumer asset like a throwaway camera or toothbrush, where one tries to obtain reasonable value for the lowest price. Fortunately, when I graduated from high school, socialism wasn't yet a discredited practice. The college closest to my home, Aspiration College, adopted an admission policy, aptly named Open Admission, that offered free admission to anyone who wanted to enter. No essays were required, no SAT test scores needed, no high school transcripts demanded, no extensive applications submitted. In fact, the Admissions Office went out of its way to ignore how poorly one may have performed in high school or how intellectually challenged one might be—the educational equivalent of (and precursor to) the Don't Ask, Don't Tell policy governing gays in the military. I am not particularly enamored of socialism's principles, but they are okay with me when they produce a price with a dollar sign followed by a zero. How bad could the education be? I was certain that after four years at Aspiration College, I would be able to quote a few lines from Shakespeare and know that Plato, Socrates, and Aristotle hung out together.

Why spend tens of thousands of dollars at a high-priced institution, versus attending one for free, only to end up with the same thing, a diploma? Some will argue that the quality of the education at a top university surpasses that of the college I went to. But my school didn't lose a debate to prisoners in the Eastern New

York Correctional Facility, as Harvard did. The Harvard debaters, scrambling to defend their immoderate tuition costs, claimed the prisoners were "phenomenally intelligent and articulate." I would have said the same thing.

While searching for a major field of study, I noted that one of the fastest-growing degrees in the country—park, recreation, leisure, and fitness studies—had increased by 92 percent over a recent ten-year period. My college did not want to miss out on this hot trend, nor did I. I applied myself diligently to the leisure part of this major. The town park I co-managed after graduation didn't pay very well but made up for it in prestige. And despite the meager salary, I was able to buy, unlike many of my school-debt-laden friends who had graduated from high-tuition universities, a weekly Lotto ticket.

So how did my college do it? How did it cover the costs of providing a four-year education without receiving any money from tuition? Efficiency, mostly. Of course, New York City and New York State provided funding, after shaking down their taxpayers, but my school had to make tough choices to get the most out of the scarce funds it had. Smartly, they terminated the long-standing underwater basket-weaving course, breaking ranks with Reed College and Rutgers University, and replaced it with an above-water version, enabling them to cut down on the use and cost of chlorine tablets. They also cut back on student amenities such as the on-campus condom ambulance services, made popular by the College of New Jersey. This forced me and thousands of other students, during the permissive sixties, to walk a block off campus to the twenty-four-hour drugstore.

Not surprisingly, an open admissions policy successfully attracts high school graduates denied admission to every other college they have chosen. The scholars that Aspiration College had assembled as my freshman class fell considerably short on a *National Geographic* survey of high school seniors, 40 percent of whom could not name the ocean on the east coast of the United States. Before anyone in my American History 101 class could answer: Who was the first president of the United States?—a question which in an Oklahoma high school only one in four students could answer—my teacher had to first explain the definition of the term president, and for the students in the back, the meaning of the United States.

Professors at Aspiration taught their course material at a pace calibrated to accommodate the less-than-nimble students who are attracted by the forward-thinking policy of Open Admissions, a pace that made poured molasses seem like running water. But after a class or two, I noted that most of the teachers were intellectually indistinguishable from the students. It was painful to listen to either, both of whom spoke as if the word street included the letter h after the s. One day, to my surprise, I met a very interesting and intelligent professor, whom I didn't see again. I learned later that he was at Aspiration that day because he had gotten off at the wrong subway stop.

If a classroom with bright, engaged students and a dynamic professor with an exciting, fast-paced teaching style accelerates the absorption of new knowledge, then my classes at Aspiration were equivalent to drilling small holes in the cranial membrane causing seepage of fluids and gray matter and the permanent loss of any knowledge that may have been attached to the discharge. At the end of my four years there, I had myself tested for IQ degeneration and, fearing a far worse outcome, was relieved to find that I had lost only fifteen IQ points.

My freshman class was as ethnically diverse as it was intellectually the same. A melting pot that hadn't quite melted, the freshmen were immigrants and first-generation young men and women from Western Europe, Eastern Europe, Asia, and South America. Broken English was the accepted language in the classroom.

The little things I remember about our college life have led me to develop a fondness for many of my classmates. On the first day of sociology class, when the professor said that we would be covering Mendel's gene theory, Gene Sokolowski thinking he had been called on, snapped out of a daydream—more like a sound sleep—with a start and asked the professor to repeat the question. I recall the time our English Lit professor introduced *The Grapes of Wrath* by John Steinbeck, and Stavros Demothenous dropped the class, thinking he had mistakenly registered for an enology course. He told his friend Luigi Abatangelo, a Gallo and Thunderbird aficionado, who promptly dropped his astronomy course and was seated next to me in English Lit the following day, eager to learn about grapes. I also remember Kiernan O'Malley, upon hearing the Bill of Rights mentioned in American history, getting upset thinking that he would now be receiving a bill for tuition, which he had thought was free. And of course there was Anthony "Fat Tony" Carlucci whom I was certain was attending our biology class as part of an adult continuing education program. Anthony—nobody dared call him "Fat Tony"—never said much in class, but he perked up when we began covering cell theory. Responding to the professor's question about the characteristics of cells, Anthony said that they were cramped, the beds were hard, and that you normally had to share it with another person. But my favorite by far was Vladimir Kalashnikov. Vlad, strong as an ox and almost as smart, aced advanced weightlifting but had trouble with geography. He insisted that the Indian Ocean was named after Chiefs Sitting Bull and Standing Bear.

Although college seemed to drag on for more than four years, and for many it did, graduation day eventually arrived. The air was warm, and the sun shone brightly, but only one hundred or so graduates, out of the total graduating class of twelve hundred, attended. Most people attributed that to a lack of interest and school spirit, but many of my fellow graduates insisted there had been a mix-up. They told me they had mistakenly received, and ignored, a commencement notice, which should have gone to the freshmen starting college, not to the seniors finishing it.

• • •

COLD
TURKEY

Headline writing, like brain surgery, should be done carefully. An imprecise headline, overlooked by an inattentive editor, although not as consequential as similar behavior by a surgeon, will embarrass those in charge of a newspaper or blog. Its readership, paralyzed by laughter, will not complain. Below is a recent headline followed by the story one might expect to be attached to it.

DACO Cracks Down on Underweight Turkeys

DACO, Puerto Rico's fierce and committed consumer-protection agency, cannot abide skinny turkeys who fall short on the ideal-weight fowl charts. The problem, it contends, is as old as the pilgrims. Unapologetic about its aggressive intervention, DACO will be sending its foot soldiers into the field to forcibly grab the thin necks of these feathery birds and pour additional amounts of feed down their throats. And if results aren't forthcoming quickly, DACO will add crushed McDonald's supersized Happy Meals to the mix. Precautions, of course, will be taken to ensure that only non-GMO ingredients are used. At the same time, more senior, experienced DACO agents will work with underweight turkeys, impressing upon them that gobble gobble isn't simply about calling for a mate, but is a term that must be applied to the way they eat.

DACO takes its consumer rights safeguarding responsibility seriously. It pledged to protect the rights of the extensive and growing number of obese consumers, estimated at 30 percent of the population in the most recent 2014 survey, by ensuring that they receive ample portions of chubby turkeys on their Thanksgiving plates. Twenty years ago, when obesity rates were much lower, lightweight turkeys were far less of an issue. Credit to DACO for recognizing this rapidly changing trend. Unwilling to stop at turkey remediation, the indefatigable agency has already announced its intentions to crack down next on stuffing.

Underweight turkeys aren't taking this lying down. In fact, they rarely lie down because sedentary habits often lead to weight gain. They are defending their right to choose their individual lifestyle preferences. They cite the overwhelming influence of skinny Barbie-like turkey models on these choices and defend their right to choose by raising the emotionally charged preference of consumers for white meat over dark.

The feathered nibblers have become more vocal about pursuing a presidential pardon, but DACO appears unworried, since Puerto Rico is a commonwealth whose citizens do not have the right to vote for president. Rumors that the turkeys will be tampering with their own tryptophan levels was, however, alarming to DACO officials, who worried that this sleep-inducing hormone might render officials sluggish after Thanksgiving and jeopardize their future consumer-protection efforts.

As it turns out, when the DACO personnel did disperse into the field, they discovered that most of the turkeys were already dead and frozen, making their ability to crack down on the underweight ones that much more challenging.

• • •

YALE
~~BULLDOGS~~ POODLES

Yale University's endowment faces trouble, now that the school has added 5,453 facilitators to its payroll, one assigned to each undergraduate student. These ~~babysitters~~ facilitators will accompany each student 24/7. The only exception is bathroom and shower breaks provided there are no other human beings present.

The university has directed each facilitator to make college "a cocoon place of comfort" for the student to whom they have been assigned and to be particularly vigilant about warding off anything their student finds offensive. Students made it clear to the administration that they were psychologically incapable of ignoring Halloween costumes and had to be protected from any frightful observations of them. Yale University's dean, pointing out that the students were exactly right, reminded the facilitators to check under the students' beds before tucking them in at night. One of Yale's professors foolishly suggested to students, "If you don't like a costume someone is wearing, look away, or tell them you are offended. Talk to each other. Free speech and the ability to tolerate offense are the hallmarks of a free and open society."

Student protesters, via their spokesperson, pointed out just how foolish that suggestion was. "We were told to meet the offensive parties head on, without suggesting any modes or means to facilitate these discussions to promote understanding."

Enter the facilitators. No longer will two students lunching together with their facilitators have to directly ask the other one to pass the ketchup. In the classroom, each student facilitator will attend class along with an assigned student. Because seating space is limited, the facilitator will sit in the seat while the student will settle in on his or her lap.

Professors will be prohibited from speaking directly to students lest one of their utterances be deemed offensive by any student having a bad-hair day. Instead, the professors must address the lesson, a sentence at a time, to the facilitators while the students hold their hands to their ears. After each sentence, the facilitators vote on whether the professor's sentence is allowable. Only after a unanimous vote "yes" are the students told to drop their hands and listen to the professor's words.

Teaching the syllabus may take a little longer. This is just a small price to pay for hermetically sealing students from controversial sentences, thoughts, or concepts, lurking in the hallways of academe, waiting to pounce on the vulnerable psyches of unwitting undergraduates and leaving psychological anguish and scarring in their wake.

Imagine the emotional bruising caused by being forced to listen to Timothy 2:11-12 in Bible studies: *"Let a woman learn quietly with all submissiveness. I do not permit a woman to teach or to exercise authority over a man; rather, she is to remain quiet."* Or a statement by Booker T. Washington in Humanities class: *"There is another class of coloured people who make a business of keeping the troubles, the wrongs and the hardships of the Negro race before the public."* Or a professor accidentally using emotionally charged words—*chairman, management, manhole cover, gingerbread man*—in one of their lectures. Or a teacher saying *Christmas tree* instead of *Holiday tree*. Or a professor so bereft of sensitivity that he might encourage a discussion of such topics as *global warming* or *reverse discrimination*. Thank God these kids are in college and no longer have to confront, with their newly acquired sense of outrage, the insensitivity, for example, of the author of Georgie Porgie—presumably Mother Goose—whose intolerant and condescending message is unmistakable when revealing that Georgie kissed girls and ran away from boys.

At Yale sporting events, where the cheers of opposing fans against the Yale team and its student supporters are downright debilitating, the facilitators, after distributing earplugs to the students in their care, will be expected to file criminal charges with the local police after the game. And all on-campus tailgating barbecues serving hamburgers and frankfurters will be permanently banned so as not to offend students of German descent, and, to be on the safe side, students descended from any of the neighboring countries.

Back to that insensitive professor and his perplexing and hurtful recommendations that students talk to each other. No, said many students. Until Halloween masks are banned from campus, Yale will not feel like home. Home was where these students presumably learned tolerance, civility, and respect for authority.

The professor got a glimpse of that upbringing when approached by a group of protesting students, one of whom tenderly told him: "You should not sleep at night. You are disgusting." Now, it is clear why facilitators and perhaps some behavior modification experts are needed.

The administration, perceptively concluding that the students were unable to manage the Halloween-costume issue, banned specific costumes and masks from campus, including sombreros and Rastafarian wigs. Missing from the banned list were baseball hats, belts embroidered with sailboats, and pastel-colored pants, long and short, with little whales on them.

The White Anglo-Saxon Protestant (WASP) community at the school marched to the president's office to convey the torment they felt from other students dressing as preppies. They found the use of these costumes offensive and degrading to the American culture and people. They, like the students who criticized the professor, were worried "about the violence that grows out of wearing offensive costumes is not something we can ignore." Inexplicably, the administration was not taking the WASP protesters seriously. The WASPs were soon being shouted down by a growing crowd of the original, bona fide, card-carrying student protestors—until one of the card carriers, a member of the Save a Whale Society, expressed the anguish she felt at the debasement of whales when people wore shorts and slacks with whales on them during Halloween. The administration capitulated and banned clothing with whale designs not only for Halloween but for the foreseeable future.

But we learned about the real crime from a well-reasoned editorial in a student campus publication. The professor's suggestion, reads the editorial, "is tainted by her decision to email it directly to all Silliman [a college at Yale] students—an email list to which she has access through her administrative role in the college. She could have published these thoughts on a personal blog or in a publication. She chose not to."

The Yale president, a quick study, learned from this editorial that it is the medium, not the message, that offends his students. He immediately changed the school's communication policy. Henceforth, the school would communicate with its seniors (presumably mature enough to deal with the threatening nature of email) by email, juniors by Twitter, sophomores by Instagram, and with freshmen, the administration would communicate using large blocks with brightly colored letters.

• • •

EU CAN'T
BE SERIOUS

The wisdom of Yogi Berra—"You better cut the pizza into four pieces because I am not hungry enough to eat six"—now has competition from the officials of the European Union, or more precisely the Orwellian-sounding European Food Safety Authority (EFSA). The producers of bottled water in Europe applied to EFSA for approval to include the statement "Regular consumption of significant amounts of water can reduce the risk of development of dehydration" on the label of their bottles.

Not so fast, said the mandarins over at EFSA, mindful that they, like Yogi, don't want to "make too many wrong mistakes." So, they studied this esoteric topic for three years, (no, that is not a typo) and with a flourish, organized a meeting with twenty-one scientists, handpicked for their deep knowledge of thirst, in Parma, Italy (the Osso buco alla Milanese shouldn't be missed). They concluded that "reduced water content in the body was a symptom of dehydration and not something that drinking water could subsequently control"—a dose of circular logic which makes Yogi's "You wouldn't have won if we'd beaten you" seem Aristotelian. Dressing up their conclusion into proper European Union bureaucratese, the EFSA apparatchiks declaimed that the proposed statement did not comply with Article 14 of Regulation (EC) No 1924/2006, and therefore producers of bottled water are forbidden, by law, from making that assertion. In light of this new scientific discovery, the EFSA group immediately began work on an EU directive banning water stations at all long-distance running races in Europe, mandating that potato chips be served instead. Unfortunately, there wasn't enough time or Osso buco left to complete their work, so another conference will have to be scheduled.

A group of year six students from Cumberland Primary School in South England, replaced the EFSA explanation of hydration with the standard dictionary definition and were confused by the result: "Reduced water content in the body was a symptom of reduced water content in the body and not something that drinking water could subsequently control."

All this work made the students thirsty, which they successfully addressed with a trip to the water fountain. One of the older students, Nigel, believed to be twelve years of age, sent a letter to the EFSA shamans asking if they felt the same way about air: reduced air in the lungs was a symptom of asphyxiation and not something that breathing could control. Nigel received a prompt and very cordial response from EFSA saying that to answer his question, they would need three years of study and another conference in Parma, Italy.

The industrious students at Cumberland did some additional research and learned that people who live at high altitudes face a greater risk of dehydration. They discovered that the mountain people of Tibet, who probably don't have a lot of bottled water with labels encouraging them to drink water to prevent dehydration, drink thirty to fifty cups a day of their national drink called Po Cha, or buttered tea, a delightful mix of yak butter, tea, and salt. Nigel presented this information in another letter to the EFSA eggheads and asked if this would change their views on hydration in any way. No, came the answer in a second courteous letter from EFSA, but with immediate effect, the European Commission was removing bottled water from the on-premises refrigerators serving its 60,000 employees and replacing it with eight-ounce cartons of Po Cha.

Those 60,000 people have been very busy, issuing directives—50,000 of them at last count—to harmonize and regulate anything that makes eye contact. And no subject is too complex for this army of subject matter experts. The EU commissioners, proud of the team they have assembled, look forward to any challenge, knowing that "we have deep depth," as Yogi would say. The European Commission has issued ten directives regulating duvets, thirty-nine for sheets, thirty-one for toothbrushes, 172 for mirrors, 118 for shampoos, 454 for towels, 1,246 for bread, fifty-two for toasters, 12,653 for milk, ninety-nine for bowls, 210 for spoons, five for pillowcases, 109 for pillows, and 225 for eyeglasses. And, for the privilege of allowing these productivity-sapping directives to smother their economy, Great Britain pays seventeen billion pounds to the EU and receives six billion pounds of benefits in return. The British almost seem like Bridiots for not Brexiting Brefore 2016.

What regulations could possibly come next—for prunes? Well, yes. Those pesky people in the private sector wishing to market and sell their prunes thought it might be a good idea to remind consumers that prunes help maintain and/or improve normal bowel function. But, before something as controversial as this could be included on a label, the EFSA scatologists would have to conduct a study. They defined improved bowel function as "reduced transit time, increased frequency of bowel movements or increased stool bulk." Right away some clarification was needed. Did "reduced transit time" mean that the consumer of prunes would take less time getting to the bathroom, or did it mean that the bulked-up stool would take less time to travel through the intestines? Either way, the EFSA scatologists had a complex measurement task before them.

Undaunted, they hired several dozen human subjects, men and women and then cleared a large area where they set up a sufficient number of EU-approved toilet bowls. They fed the subjects large quantities of prunes, and with EU-approved stopwatches began timing the stools' journeys, taking extra precautions not to tell the subjects to push, otherwise the results might be tainted.

Further details on research methodology and results remain murky, but EFSA concluded that "the evidence is insufficient to establish a cause-and-effect relationship between the consumption of prunes and maintenance of normal bowel function" [*EFSA Journal* 2010; 8(2): 1486]. Copies of the opinion will be sent to the Cumberland Primary School, where the young students who did such fine work on bottled water, will read this new pronouncement from EFSA and understand what Yogi meant when he said, "It's like déjà vu all over again."

• • •

EPILOGUE

Mandatory retirement encroached on my rapid journey from Queens into the fast lane. For goodness sake, I was already on the service road of life's highway; just a few more lanes to go before I would be cruising along, opening up the throttle with society's elite. If I just had a little more time.

However, the retirement party in the back room of the Kiwanis Club beckoned, with laminated folding tables decoratively covered with paper tablecloths, and the peeling, red cloth wallpaper almost unnoticeably re-adhered to the wall behind it. The party was well attended by easily more than a dozen people, all enjoying their drinks in plastic cups from the first-drink-free bar. Heck, even the assistant vice president of operations showed up to present me with a Casio watch for my thirty years of service.

That seemed liked years ago. Celebrations over, I have downshifted, returning to the slower moving traffic in life's right lane, more accurately, the side streets. These days, a major accomplishment for me is remaining awake for an entire full-length movie. The experts recommend engaging in a sport or a hobby. I never had an interest in golf, and have reluctantly concluded that I am too old to take up bobsledding or pole vaulting. I thought about resuming my stamp collecting, but I can't remember where I put my album.

With all the extra free time, I am making a lot of new friends and am seeing many old friends more often: my dentist, internist, cardiologist, urologist, optometrist, ophthalmologist, gastroenterologist, and of course my psychologist and psychiatrist.

Whoever called these the golden years hadn't reached them yet.

I lamented to my psychiatrist that I have been seeing him for forty-six years and have still not been cured. He says I am making great progress, but that therapy takes time and cannot be rushed. I heard him mumble something about my being more than halfway through the treatment program, which would put me in tiptop mental health at age 110. I guess he has mouths at home to feed, or based on the exorbitant fees he charges me, heirs to provide for.

My wife, Diane, insisted that now I am retired, and with all four of our children finished with college and out of the house, we should eat out often and travel the world. I gently reminded her that when our children left the house for college, the bulk of our savings left the house at the same time. I encouraged her to read the AARP magazine that began arriving bimonthly, particularly the articles explaining the risks of being on a fixed income and the inadequacies of social security payments.

She would have none of it.

So, we eat out often. And travel often. To make it work financially, I have discovered all the Early Bird (dinner) Specials offered by any restaurant with a twenty-mile radius. We eat dinner at 3:30 and go to sleep at 6pm to make sure we don't get hungry again in the evening. Diane and I had different notions of travel. While I thought we should drive to the neighboring towns we hadn't seen in a long time, Diane thought we should fly to neighboring hemispheres we hadn't seen at all. Fortunately, I found some sizable discounts on Ukraine Air, where each flight has nearly enough seats for all its passengers. Mental health gurus and motivational speakers preach that money will buy style and comfort, but it will not buy happiness. I sure would be happier if my bank account balance weren't declining as fast as it is.

The pace of social and technological change over the course of my life has stunned me.

When I went to college, students were expected to confront and discuss controversial ideas, and feel some pressure to get good grades. Everyone loved Halloween. Back then, a safe space was the painted path on a street where a crossing guard helped young children cross from one side to the other. Now? I am still having it explained to me but a safe space (a location on campus where students can go to avoid ideas and speech that make them feel uncomfortable) sure sounds like I place that I would have much preferred to be than in a classroom with a boring professor. And to think that decision would be up to me since I could I issue a trigger warning---an alert that warns others that my sensibilities are being offended---to that boring professor to back off if he threatened to penalize me for not attending his class. Having Halloween subjected to cultural appropriation taboos would have been a bummer, though. Removing nearly all costume creativity would have made for a dull holiday celebration.

I also remember when ADD was something we did in arithmetic class. In fourth grade, we knew little Tommy McCusker as a boy who never stopped running during recess (and sometimes during class) and couldn't seem to understand the multiplication tables. Back then, no one understood much about Attention Deficit Disorder, but I always made sure that I chose Tommy for my side when we played team tag.

There was a time in my life when Tweet was the sound a bird made, and Snap was a movement made with my fingers when I heard a sweet-sounding tune. In my early years, I recall having a tough time mastering the use of the three knobs on our brand-new color television set compared with the two on our black-and-white one. What chance do I have now with the bewildering number of buttons on the TV remote control and the plethora of channels, streaming videos, YouTube and Hulus (whatever that is) available? It drives me crazy and makes me schedule extra appointments with my impecunious psychiatrist.

Soon we will have a President who tweets, and a machine that we can ask questions of. Oh, we already have that.

"Alexa, how many steps have I walked today, and who is going to win the fifth race at Belmont tomorrow?"

· · ·

ROBERT J. LICALZI

Bob was born and raised in Queens, NY, where his fondest childhood memories were the invention of color television and his first day as a teenager, when, after twelve sweltering summers, his father bought an air conditioner to cool the family apartment. After graduating from Queens College, Bob began working for an international bank.

A few years later, in the late 1970s, the bank assigned Bob to sunny Puerto Rico at a time when sunblock did not have numbers. There, Bob met and married Diane. After job assignments in Tokyo, London, and New York, and after having four children, Bob retired from the bank, moved the family to Puerto Rico, and learned the importance of SPFs (Sun Protection Factors).

Bob has been an aspiring writer ever since his choice of Finance over Journalism as a major in college temporarily postponed that aspiration until the room was cleared after his retirement party. Bob has written hundreds of opinion pieces and briefly ran a blog called "Puerto Rico Commentary," which presented his views of Puerto Rico's economic policies. He was encouraged to publish this collection of essays, mostly by his children who, while still on allowance, found every one of them funny.

CPSIA information can be obtained
at www.ICGtesting.com
Printed in the USA
BVHW07s2200180718
521943BV00014B/841/P

9 781944 515553